Homemade Liqueurs and Infused Spirits

HOMEMADE
Liqueurs and
INFUSED SPIRITS

Innovative Flavor Combinations, plus Homemade Versions of Kahlúa, Cointreau & Other Popular Liqueurs

ANDREW SCHLOSS

Photography by Leigh Beisch

Storey Publishing

Dedicated to The Symposium for Professional Food Writers,
where I learned to drink

The mission of Storey Publishing is to serve our customers by
publishing practical information that encourages
personal independence in harmony with the environment.

Edited by Margaret Sutherland and Lisa Hiley
Art direction and book design by Jessica Armstrong
Text production by Jennifer Jepson Smith

Photography by © Leigh Beisch Photography, except:
Popular Science Monthly Volume 51/Wikimedia
Commons, 12; © Colin Soutar/iStockphoto.com, 15;
Courtesy of Digital Collections, East Carolina
University, 104; © SSPL/David Nathan-Maister/Getty
Images, 106; Courtesy of Harvard College Library
Imaging Services, 232; © Evgeny Karandaev/123RF.
com, 236 (all except top row right) and 237;
© jarp5/123RF.com, 236 (top row right); and
© Karen Shain Schloss back cover, author photo

Indexed by Nancy D. Wood

Storey books are available for special premium and
promotional uses and for customized editions. For
further information, please call 1-800-793-9396.

Storey Publishing
210 MASS MoCA Way
North Adams, MA 01247
www.storey.com

Printed in China by Toppan Leefung Printing Ltd.
10 9 8 7 6 5 4 3 2 1

LIBRARY OF CONGRESS CATALOGING-IN-PUBLICATION DATA

Schloss, Andrew, 1951–
   Homemade liqueurs and infused spirits / by Andrew
Schloss.
      pages cm
   Includes index.
   ISBN 978-1-61212-098-0 (pbk. : alk. paper)
   ISBN 978-1-60342-883-5 (ebook)
   1. Liqueurs. I. Title.
TP611.S35 2013
663'.55—dc23
                                         2013009929

Storey Publishing is committed to making
environmentally responsible manufacturing
decisions. This book was printed on paper
made from sustainably harvested fiber.

CONTENTS

ACKNOWLEDGMENTS

I never realized what a lazy writer I could be until I started testing inebriants. Working on this book has been a blast for me but, I fear, a slog for the editors, designers, agents, and publisher forced to whip me into meeting my deadlines. If you appreciate this book at all, you are as indebted to their diligence as I am. They are Lisa Ekus, book agent; Margaret Sutherland, acquiring editor; and most of all Lisa Hiley, the editor and superego of everything you see before you. Thanks also to Valerie Cimino, who copy-edited the text, Jessica Armstrong, who designed the pages, and Leigh Beisch and Dan Becker, the photographer and photo stylist, who found innumerable props and compositions to make a glass and a bottle of booze look scrumptious every time.

Preface

Of all the potent potables that one can brew at home, liqueurs are the fastest, easiest, and most versatile. Liqueurs are liquors (distilled spirits) that have been flavored with sugar and aromatics, such as herbs, spices, nuts, flowers, fruits, seeds, vegetables, roots, and/or bark.

The practice of infusing alcohol with other ingredients began as a way of making herbal medicines. Cordials were liqueurs that stimulated circulation — the word "cordial" comes from the Latin *cor*, meaning "heart."

The same chemical properties that give alcohol the ability to bind with medicinal elements in herbs and spices also make it bind with tastes and aromas. By the fifteenth century, liqueurs had moved from the pharmacy to the dining room, where they were served to enhance food. Liqueurs served before eating (aperitifs) set up the appetite for the main courses to come. Those served after the meal (digestifs) helped one digest what had already been consumed.

Liqueurs can be flavored by soaking flavorful ingredients in already distilled alcohol, a process known as tincturing, or by distilling them along with the alcohol. Those made by tincture are easier to fabricate and tend to be sweeter and more viscous than those that are made by distilling the flavorings and alcohol together. The tincture method is not only the easier of the two; currently it is the only method that is legal in North America.

The popularity of home-brewing beer and wine has given rise to an interest in artisan moonshining (home distilling). New Zealand repealed its ban on home distillation in 1996, and distillation for home use is not outlawed in countries that have a long cultural history of small scale home-based artisan stills, like Italy and Ukraine, but in the United States and Canada, distilling without a license is still illegal.*

Homebrewing and winemaking require a laboratory of equipment, a repertoire of special skills, and weeks to years of time and patience to produce something drinkable — not so liqueurs. A modestly equipped kitchen provides all of the tools necessary for making almost any liqueur, and provided your interest is centered on fabricating libation, rather than medication, most any liqueur can be made in a matter of days, and some as quickly as a few hours.

✱ HR Bill 3949, introduced in the 110th Congress on October 23, 2007, by Representative Bart Stupak of Michigan, attempted to amend the Internal Revenue Code to repeal the prohibition on producing distilled spirits in specified locations, including dwelling houses and enclosed areas connected with any dwelling house. The bill died in committee.

1

The Basics

Homemade Liqueurs & Tasteful Spirits

Flavoring alcohol is straightforward. Most liqueurs use neutral grain alcohol, such as vodka, as a base, although I use a variety of bases, including rum, tequila, whiskey, vermouth, and wine. The process of infusing such nonvolatile substances as iodine into alcohol in the preparation of medications is known as tincturing. Even though liqueurs are no longer considered medicinal, I find it clarifying to use this somewhat archaic term to describe the process of flavoring spirits.

To make a tincture, the flavoring ingredients are broken or cut into small pieces to expose more surface area to the alcohol, and sometimes sugar syrup is added with them. I have found that adding sugar in the initial stages of tincturing slows down the transfer of flavorful components into the alcohol. So when using a flavorful sugar such as brown sugar, agave, jaggery, or honey, which has aromatic elements that need to infuse into the liquor base, I add the sweetener in the first step, but when using unflavored sugar syrup made from granulated white sugar, I add the sugar after the initial tincturing is complete.

When the flavoring ingredients are combined with the alcohol, the chemical power of alcohol takes over. Alcohol bonds with both water-soluble and fat-soluble molecules, which gives it awesome power to attract and hold on to any flavor molecules. Those flavors perceived on the tongue (salty, sweet, sour, bitter, and umami) are soluble in water, while all other flavors (herbal, fruity, spicy, floral, garlicky, and so on) are fat soluble and perceived through the nose.

When you are flavoring a recipe, your cooking medium largely determines what flavors emerge. Boil garlic in water and the results are largely sweet. Sauté the same amount of garlic in oil and the sugars are unnoticeable, but the garlicky pungency can be overwhelming. But soak a flavorful ingredient in alcohol and the solubility of its flavorful components doesn't matter: Everything ends up in the booze.

Different ingredients take more or less time to infuse their flavors into an alcohol base. The timing depends on several factors:

* The **proof** (alcohol percentage) of the base spirit

* The **concentration** of flavorful components in the blend

* The **volatility** of the flavorful components

PROOF. The concept of proof developed in the eighteenth century, when British sailors were paid partly in rum. To ensure that the rum had not been watered down, it was

BASIC BOOZE VOCABULARY

▶ **ALCOHOL BY VOLUME (ABV).** Percentage of alcohol in a solution in volume measure

▶ **BREW.** To prepare beer by steeping or infusing water with grains and hops and fermenting the resulting mash

▶ **DISTILL.** To vaporize a liquid, such as alcohol, and cool the resulting gas to precipitate a purer form of the liquid

▶ **FERMENT.** To convert sugar into carbon dioxide and alcohol using yeast

▶ **INFUSE.** To permeate a fluid with elements from a solid material

▶ **LIQUEUR.** A flavorful sweet distilled spirit

▶ **LIQUOR.** An alcoholic beverage

▶ **PROOF.** A numerical description of the percentage of alcohol in a liquid equal to about half of the actual ABV

▶ **STEEP.** To infuse in water

▶ **TINCTURE.** To infuse in alcohol

"proved" to be undiluted by dousing gunpowder with the liquor, then testing to see if the gunpowder would ignite. If it wouldn't, the alcohol content was considered too low, or underproof. A proven solution was defined as 100 degrees proof, because it was assumed that it did not contain any water.

It was later found that rum-doused gunpowder would ignite as long as the rum had more than 57 percent alcohol by volume. Expressed as a ratio, 57 percent is roughly 7:4. So 70 proof liquor had about 40 percent alcohol by volume. Later this was rounded to a ratio of 8:4, or 2:1.

As you can see, proof is only an approximate measure of a liquor's alcohol content. It is not permitted as a legal measure of the amount of alcohol produced through distillation. Although a liquor label may state the proof of its contents, it must also state the alcohol content as a percentage of volume (ABV).

HANDY PROOF CHART

80 proof	40% alcohol
90 proof	45% alcohol
100 proof	50% alcohol
140 proof	70% alcohol
190 proof	95% alcohol

The higher the proof of the alcohol base, the faster it captures flavoring components from added ingredients. Most whiskeys and rums are 80 proof. Gins can be 80 or 86 proof, and several vodkas reach 140 proof. Everclear is the highest-proof commercial spirit, topping out at 190 proof.

CONCENTRATION. Drier ingredients, like dehydrated fruits and dried spices and herbs, have more concentrated flavoring elements because their water content has been reduced. Their fresh counterparts contain up to 60 percent less flavor molecules by weight and therefore need much more time to fully flavor an alcohol base.

Concentrated ingredients like dried cherries might take a couple of days to infuse, while fresh cherries would require a week or more in alcohol to release the same amount of flavor. That said, using finely shredded fresh fruits and vegetables produces a lighter, more natural-tasting liqueur than one made solely from dehydrated produce.

VOLATILITY. Some flavoring compounds disperse more easily than others, which is why certain ingredients smell more intense than others. A cracked cinnamon stick or a split vanilla bean will release its flavor into a bottle of brandy in about 24 hours. Pungent aromatic ingredients like horseradish or black pepper can flavor a fifth of vodka in just a few hours.

FLAVORING
AGENTS

Tincturing to Taste

Every recipe in this book gives a range of tincturing time. Take a taste at the earliest end and let it go longer if the tincture is not as flavorful as you like. It is best to not let the tincturing go longer than the recommended time; longer isn't always better.

The first flavors to be released into the base are the most volatile, lightest, and freshest-tasting ones. After a while, heavier tannic and bitter flavors will start to emerge. Usually these flavors are undesirable, so the mixture should be drained before they develop.

When the desired flavor is reached, the solid ingredients are strained from the liquid. Try to avoid the tendency to press on the ingredients in an attempt to extract the ultimate amount of liquid. True, you can get a better yield by applying some force, but you can also force small solid particles into the alcohol, which will cause cloudiness in the finished liqueur.

Once the solid ingredients have been separated, they can be discarded (although dried fruit that has been marinating in alcohol makes a delicious garnish for ice cream). Sugar syrup is added to the flavored liquor as a last step in its transformation into liqueur. The amount is largely up to personal taste, but generally 33 to 50 percent of the volume of alcohol will yield the best results.

The more sugar syrup added to the alcohol base, the silkier the mouthfeel of the finished liqueur will be. This viscosity slows down the flow of the liqueur across your palate, which allows the liqueur to linger in your mouth longer, thereby giving your taste buds and olfactory receptors more time to pick up flavor, which is why sweeter liquids taste more intense than thinner ones. (It is also why "watery" can describe both the flavor and the consistency of a food or beverage.)

Sugar syrup is easy to make and keeps for several weeks in the refrigerator. I prepare several types to have on hand for flavoring and coloring liqueurs, including Brown Simple Syrup, Caramelized Simple Syrup, and four types of creamy sugar syrups for cream liqueurs: Creamy Simple Syrup, Brown Cow Simple Syrup, Tangy-Creamy Simple Syrup, and Coconut Cream Simple Syrup (see recipes starting on page 24).

Once completed, most liqueurs will keep their flavor and color for about a year if stored in a tightly closed container in a cool, dark location. Cream liqueurs need to be refrigerated, and they will keep for at least a month. Cream liqueurs have a tendency to separate as they sit because the fat in the cream rises to the top. They can be recombined by shaking before serving.

► **CLOCKWISE FROM TOP LEFT:** *Maple Syrup (page 214), Herb-Santé (page 108), Blueberry Cinnamon (page 40), Elderflower Blush (page 164), Red Lightning (page 92), and Cucumber Gin (page 226)*

JUST TO BE CLEAR

I am not a stickler for crystal clarity, and so most of the time I simply strain out the solids from the tinctured liqueur and call it a day. But some liqueurs throw off sediment as they sit. If you want to remove that sediment, there are two methods.

FILTERING. Line a strainer with two or three layers of damp cheesecloth; set over a clean jar and slowly pour the liqueur through it. Try to avoid pouring the sediment in the bottom of the jar into the strainer.

RACKING. Place a clean jar or bottle in a deep kitchen sink. Set the jar of liqueur on the counter next to the sink. The bottom of the full jar must be higher than the top of the empty container. If necessary, set the jar of liqueur on an overturned pot.

Stick one end of a 3- or 4-foot length of clean, flexible plastic tubing (the tubing used in an aquarium is perfect) into the liqueur, making sure that the submerged tip of the tube is well above the sediment in the bottom of the jar. Suck on the other end of the tube until alcohol flows almost to the end, then quickly tuck the end into the empty bottle. The liqueur will flow from the jar into the bottle, leaving the sediment behind.

▶ **FOR THE CLEAREST RESULTS,** *don't press on the flavoring agents to squeeze out every last drop when straining the liqueur. You may garner a couple more mouthfuls of liquid, but you'll also wind up with some cloudiness from small particles. Shown here is Raspberry Rose (page 156).*

TYPES OF LIQUEURS

Liqueurs are grouped by how they are flavored, as shown in this listing of popular commercial brands. The chapters in the book follow these groupings, with recipes ranging from highly inventive originals to copycats of commercial formulas (highlighted in blue). Although it is impossible to replicate secret corporate formulas exactly, most of the copycat recipes included come fairly close.

FRUIT LIQUEURS

* Amabili *(banana)*
* Apricot *(apricot)*
* Bajtra *(prickly pear)*
* Chambord *(raspberry)*
* Cherry Heering *(sweet cherries)*
* Cointreau *(orange)*
* Curaçao *(bitter orange)*
* Gran Torres *(orange peel)*
* Grand Marnier *(brandy and orange)*
* Grapèro *(pink grapefruit)*
* Guavaberry *(guava)*
* Guignolet *(wild cherries)*
* Hare Vişne *(sour cherries)*
* Hypnotiq *(tropical blend)*
* Kruškovac *(pear)*
* Lichido *(lychee)*
* Lillehammer *(lingonberry)*
* Limoncello *(lemon)*
* Mandarine Napoléon *(brandy and mandarin orange)*
* Manzana Verde or Apple Pucker *(green apple)*
* Midori *(melon)*
* Passoã *(passion fruit, mango, pineapple, coconut)*
* Pisang Ambon *(banana)*
* Prunelle *(plum)*
* Sloe gin *(sloe berries or buckthorn plums)*
* Southern Comfort *(whiskey, peach, orange)*
* Triple sec *(orange)*

VEGETABLE LIQUEURS

* Cynar *(artichoke)*
* Rhubarb *(rhubarb)*

HERB LIQUEURS

* Absinthe *(anise, fennel, hyssop, peppermint, wormwood leaves)*
* Anisette *(anise seed)*
* Bénédictine *(Cognac flavored with 27 herbs)*
* Chartreuse *(flavored with 130 herbs)*
* Galliano *(star anise, mint, ginger)*
* Goldwasser *(a blend of roots and herbs with flakes of 23-karat gold)*
* Herbsaint *(absinthe)*
* Izarra *(yellow, made from 32 herbs and almonds, and mint-flavored green, made from 48 herbs)*
* Jägermeister *(made from 56 herbs)*
* Ouzo *(star anise, coriander, clove, cinnamon)*
* Pastis *(anise, licorice)*
* Pernod *(anise, fennel, melissa, wormwood leaves)*
* Ricard *(anise, licorice, star anise)*
* Sambuca *(anise, star anise, licorice, elderflower)*
* Strega *(made from 70 herbs, including saffron and fennel)*

NUT LIQUEURS

- **Amaretto** *(almond flavored, usually from the pits of stone fruits like apricots, peaches, and cherries)*
- **Frangelico** *(hazelnut)*
- **Kahana Royale** *(macadamia)*
- **Nocello** *(walnuts and hazelnuts)*
- **Nocino and Vin de Noix** *(unripe green walnuts)*
- **Praline** *(pecan)*

FLORAL LIQUEURS

Many blended herb liqueurs contain flower blossoms, but a few are made exclusively from flowers.

- **Crème de rose**
- **Crème de violette** *(violet)*
- **Fior D'Alpe** *(mixed wild flowers)*
- **Hypnotiq Harmonie**
- **Lavande** *(lavender)*
- **Rosolio** *(rose)*
- **Shan Hibiscus** *(hibiscus and coconut)*
- **St-Germain** *(elderflower)*
- **Xaica** *(hibiscus)*
- **Xtabentún** *(from the Yucatán, made from honey from the nectar of morning glory blossoms)*

CHOCOLATE AND COFFEE LIQUEURS

- **Afrikoko** *(chocolate and coconut)*
- **Ashanti Gold** *(dark chocolate)*
- **Chéri Suisse** *(chocolate and cherry)*
- **Kahlúa** *(dark coffee)*
- **Kona Gold** *(Kona coffee)*
- **Mozart Amadé** *(dark chocolate with blood orange)*
- **Sheridan's** *(split bottle with dark coffee and milk chocolate)*
- **Tia Maria** *(Jamaican Blue Mountain coffee)*
- **Vandermint** *(mint chocolate)*

CREAM LIQUEURS

- **Baileys Irish Cream** *(Irish whiskey and cream)*
- **Amarula** *(caramel and marula fruit)*
- **Advocaat** *(egg and vanilla)*
- **Dulce de Leche** *(caramel and cream)*
- **Mozart Gold Chocolate Cream** *(chocolate and cream)*
- **Voyant Chai Cream** *(chai, vanilla, cream)*

CARAMEL AND HONEY LIQUEURS

- **Brandymel**
- **Bruadar** *(Scotch, honey, sloe berries)*
- **Eblana** *(coffee, honey)*
- **Stag's Breath** *(single-malt Speyside Scotch, fermented honey)*
- **Yukon Jack** *(honey)*
- **Rock & Rye** *(caramelized rock sugar)*
- **Drambuie** *(honey and herbs)*
- **Wild Turkey** *(bourbon and honey)*

The Difference between Liquor and Liqueur

All liqueurs are composed of just three components: liquor (distilled spirits), flavoring, and sugar. Liquor is distilled from fermented fluids, either wine (fermented sugary liquids such as fruit juice, sugarcane juice, or elderflower juice) or beer (starchy mashes such as barley mash, rice mash, or mashed potatoes). Since alcohol boils at a lower temperature than water — 173°F (78°C) compared to 212°F (100°C) — when wine or beer are heated, more alcohol than water turns into vapor.

Liquor is made by capturing that vapor and cooling it until it returns to a liquid state. The resulting spirit has a higher alcohol content than the original beer or wine, and because aromatic chemicals are also highly volatile, it has a more concentrated flavor as well.

The art of distillation is ancient. Mesopotamians were capturing the scents of aromatic plants through distillation more than 5,000 years ago. Written documents suggest that the earliest distilled alcoholic beverages were made by the Chinese, who concentrated alcohol from fermented grain about 2,000 years ago. By the tenth century, privileged Chinese were drinking distilled alcohols, and by the thirteenth century, spirits were being sold commercially.

By 1100 alcohol distilled from wine had a reputation as a valuable medicine in Italy, and throughout Europe alchemists viewed distilled alcohol as a powerful quintessence or vaporous "fifth element" that in addition to the four basic elements (earth, water, air, and fire) made up the world.

A medieval still for making aqua vitae

ALCOHOL CONTENT OF DISTILLED LIQUORS

SPIRIT	DISTILLED ABV (PERCENT)	DISTILLED PROOF	BOTTLED ABV (PERCENT)	BOTTLED PROOF
Bourbon	60–70	120–140	40–54	80–108
Brandy	55–90	110–180	40	80
Canadian whiskey	80	160	40	80
Fruit alcohol	65–90	130–180	40	80
Gin	95	190	38–46	76–92
Irish whiskey	80	160	40–60	80–120
Rum	55–90	110–180	40–43	80–86
Scotch	70	140	40–60	80–120
Tequila	55	110	38–46	76–92
Vodka	95–96	190–192	35–50	70–100

In the early fourteenth century, the Valencian alchemist and physician Arnaldus de Villanova, in his medical book on wine, *Liber de Vinis* (the first mass-printed wine book), dubbed the essence of wine *aqua vitae*, or "water of life." The term has given name to most distilled spirits, including Scandinavian aquavit and French eau-de-vie. In English, "whiskey" is the anglicized version of the Gaelic *beatha*, "water of life." Even the term "spirit" identifies alcohol as the soul of fermentation.

Spirits distilled from wine have different characteristics from those distilled from beer. Fruit-based spirits are divided between brandy (made from grapes) and fruit alcohol (made from other fruits). Grain-based spirits are divided among single-malt whiskey (made from malted barley), whiskey and gin (made from grain and malted barley), bourbon (made from corn and malted barley plus a regulated amount of other grain), and vodka (usually made from grain, but also from potato or other starches). Rum is distilled from fermented molasses or sugarcane, and tequila and mescal are distilled from fermented agave.

Turning Liquor into Liqueur

The following are the liquors most commonly used as bases for concocting liqueurs.

BRANDY (GRAPE LIQUORS)

Brandies are distilled from grape wine. The two most prestigious are Cognac and Armagnac, the first named for a town north of Bordeaux in southwest France and the second for a region south of Bordeaux. Both are made from Trebbiano grapes, which are used to make more wine than any other grape in the world. Trebbiano grapes produce fresh, fruity, undistinguished wines that do not age well, but because of their fruitiness and high acidity, retain full flavor throughout distillation.

Cognac is double distilled with the lees still in the juice. Lees are the sediment of dead yeast that falls to the bottom of the tank after fermentation. They are quite pungent and give Cognac a savory, yeasty quality that balances the sweetness of the grape. Cognac is usually distilled to an alcohol content of 70 percent.

Armagnac is single distilled without lees to about 55 percent alcohol. The shorter fermentation time preserves more of the fruit's volatile acids, which makes Armagnac rougher and more assertive than Cognac.

By law, both Armagnac and Cognac are aged in new French oak barrels for flavor; the oak flavors dissipate as a barrel is used for a minimum of six months, but most brandies are aged for at least two years. The best Armagnac is aged for 20 years or more; Cognac can be aged for over 60 years before being bottled. Both are diluted to about 40 percent alcohol, and their flavor and color may be corrected with sugar, oak extract, and caramel before bottling.

Marc and *grappa* are the French and Italian names for single-distilled brandy made from pomace, the fermented skins, seeds, stems, and pulp left over from pressing grapes for wine. This solid debris still has some juice and a lot of sugar and tannins remaining in it, which, with the addition of water and a second period of fermentation,

yield a pungent wine. Distillation concentrates the flavor, producing a brandy that is known for its strength and sharpness.

Traditionally, marc and grappa were bottled as is, without filtering out the sharper alcohols created in the distillation process, but today more refined aged products are being produced. With age, marc and grappa can develop the same flavor chemicals as those in blue cheese, a quality that is highly prized by aficionados.

WHISKEY (BEER LIQUORS)

Distilled beer (minus the hops) is aged in wood to develop color and flavor, eventually producing whiskey. Like beer, much of its primary character depends on the mix of grains used in its preparation. Whiskeys made with all malted barley are called "single-malt." Those made with a combination of malted barley and grains are called "grain whiskey." These can be named for the type of grain used, such as rye, or they can be named for their place of origin, such as Scotch, Irish, or Canadian.

SCOTCHES, especially single-malt types, are some of the most flavorful and nuanced (and most expensive) whiskeys in the world. One of the characteristic qualities of Scotch is a smoky aroma that comes from drying the malt over a live fire. In the western and northern areas of Scotland, called the Islands and Highland region, respectively, the fuel usually includes peat, a form of dried compost that gives peat-smoked Scotch a particularly earthy character. There are two types of Scotch that are commonly available:

Single-malt Scotch is made from 100 percent malted barley, and each brand is made

A modern whiskey distillery in Scotland

at a single distillery, usually in the Highland region of Speyside or on one of the western islands of Arran, Jura, Mull, Orkney, or Skye. The Isle of Islay to the south is considered its own single-malt region. Highland single malts include Balvenie, Cragganmore, Dalmore, Glenfiddich, McClelland's, and The Glenlivet. Island single-malt distilleries include Arran, Bruichladdich, Jura, and Talisker. Laphroaig is the most popular Islay Scotch.

Blended Scotch is a blend of different single-malt and grain whiskeys that usually come from more than one distillery. This category accounts for 90 percent of the whiskey produced in Scotland. They are usually less than half single malt, and each brand has its own style. Popular blended Scotches include Dewar's, Johnnie Walker, Cutty Sark, and J&B.

Regardless of its type, by law all Scotch must be distilled in a Scottish distillery. It cannot be distilled to alcohol strength of more than 94.7 percent so that it retains the flavor of its raw materials. It must be aged in Scotland in oak barrels for at least three years. And it cannot be bottled at less than 40 percent alcohol by volume.

Scotch is typically aged in barrels that were previously used for aging wine or other liquors, to ensure that the most volatile elements in the wood have dissipated. The most common casks are sherry or bourbon casks, most typically bourbon, since there is a nearly endless supply because of U.S. regulations that bourbon must always be aged in new barrels.

Sometimes a Scotch label will specify the type of cask used. It will also tell you if the Scotch is bottled undiluted, specified as "cask strength," which is typically between 50 and 60 percent ABV. If the Scotch is single malt, the name of the distillery will be specified as well as the fact that it is single malt. If it has been cask aged for any amount of time past the minimum requirement, the number of years will be listed. The age on the label is the amount of time the Scotch spent in a barrel before bottling. If there is a date on the bottle, it is the date of the bottling.

IRISH WHISKEY. Like Scotch, Irish whiskey can be single malt, single grain, or blended. Irish whiskey has a unique classification, "pure pot still whiskey," referring to a pot or batch method of distilling rather than the column, or continuous, method. Many whiskeys are batch distilled, but the "pure pot" designation for Irish whiskey means that the liquor is made with 100 percent barley, about half of which is malted. This is different from single malt, which is also 100 percent barley, but all of that is malted.

Irish whiskeys are typically triple distilled, which makes them lighter in color and less flavorful than Scotch, and they are never cooked over peat, so they do not have a smoky character.

There are far fewer distilleries in Ireland than in Scotland. Bushmills makes both blended and single-malt whiskeys. Jameson is the primary distiller of pure pot still Irish whiskey; they also make a blended whiskey.

CANADIAN WHISKEY. Made mostly from a blend of grains, Canadian whiskey is known for its mild flavor and delicate aromas. Canadian whiskey often includes rye in its grain blend, and a few Canadian whiskeys are 100 percent rye. By law they are aged for at least three years in oak casks. The most popular brands are Canadian Club and Crown Royal. Glen Breton Rare, from Nova Scotia, is a boutique single-malt Canadian whiskey. Canadian whiskey can include small additions of other whiskeys, brandies, wine, and/ or rum, up to 9 percent of the blend.

BOURBON WHISKEY. Named for the county in Kentucky that was its birthplace, bourbon is made from corn. By law bourbon must be at least 51 percent corn, but in practice the percentage is closer to 70 percent, with the remainder a mixture of malted barley, wheat, and/or rye. Most bourbon is double distilled to an ABV of 60 to 80 percent and then aged for a minimum of two years in new charred American oak casks, which give bourbon a deep amber color and a pronounced vanilla flavor note.

Unlike French brandies and Canadian whiskeys, caramel color, sugar, and other flavorings are not permitted in bourbon production. Nothing other than grain, yeast, and water goes into a bottle of bourbon.

Although Kentucky continues to be the largest bourbon-producing state, Tennessee whiskey is similar, except that it is maple-charcoal filtered before aging, a step that gives it a distinctive flavor. The largest producer of Tennessee whiskey is Jack Daniel's. Popular Kentucky bourbons include Jim Beam, Knob Creek, Maker's Mark, Wild Turkey, and Woodford Reserve.

RYE WHISKEY. In the United States, where most rye whiskey is distilled, the formula must contain at least 51 percent rye grain. Canadian whiskey, which usually contains some rye, is sometimes referred to as rye whiskey, although Canada does not stipulate the amount of rye in whiskeys.

Rye is harsher, less sweet, and not as syrupy as bourbon, giving it a complex, and some might say coarse, flavor profile. The major producers are Jim Beam, Heaven Hill, Buffalo Trace, and Old Overholt.

VODKA

Vodka can be distilled from a fermentation of any substance high enough in carbohydrates to produce alcohol. In Russia, where it originated, vodka (which means "little water" in Russian) was made from the cheapest source available — commonly grain (sorghum, corn, rye, or wheat), potatoes, or sugar beets.

The specific base ingredient is unimportant because vodka is distilled to rid it of all aromatics and then filtered through charcoal to produce a smooth, neutral, pure spirit. Typically, vodka is continuously distilled to 95 percent ABV and bottled without further aging at around 40 percent ABV.

Because the goal of vodka is purity, filtered vodkas are the norm, although small distilleries are increasingly producing unfiltered vodkas, which have more flavor and character. Smirnoff and Stolichnaya are the most well-known Russian vodkas. Absolut and Finlandia are popular Scandinavian vodkas. Grey Goose is from France.

GIN

Gin, a neutral spirit flavored with juniper berries, comes in two styles. The most common, English-style or London dry gin, is made by diluting a double-distilled 95 percent grain spirit with water, adding juniper berries and other flavorings — most often coriander but occasionally other spices — and distilling it a third time to flavor it and return the distillation to 95 percent ABV. The distillate is diluted before bottling to between 37 and 47 percent ABV. Brands of English-style gin include Beefeater, Bombay, Boodles, Gordon's, and Tanqueray.

The Dutch method of distilling gin is made by double- or triple-distilling a fermentation of malt, corn, and rye to a fairly low alcohol level, around 30 percent. At that ABV, many flavors from fermentation are still present in the spirit. Juniper and other spices are added, and the spirit is distilled one more time to an ABV of around 40 percent. It is then bottled without further dilution. Dutch-style gins include Bols and Hendrick's. Plymouth is a Dutch style of gin that can only be made in Plymouth, England, and genever (called "Holland gin" in England) is the original Dutch gin, flavored assertively with juniper (*genièvre* is French for "juniper").

The aromatics in gin, which come from terpenes in the spices, are typically piney, citrusy, or floral. They can be subtle or pronounced, with the Dutch method producing the most flavorful gins. Some distilleries flavor their gins with scores of ingredients. Hendrick's gin, made in Scotland, is distilled with cucumber and roses; Beefeater gin contains nine herbs and spices, including juniper, angelica, and coriander, as well as licorice, almonds, and Seville oranges.

RUM

Rum contains neither fruit nor grain. It is distilled from fermented sugarcane juice or molasses, resulting in a rough alcohol that can be light or dark. Traditional dark or black rums, which come mostly from Jamaica and the French-speaking Caribbean islands, are fermented with a special yeast (*Schizosaccharomyces*) that produces a large amount of fruity-tasting esters. The fermentation is distilled in pot stills in small batches to a low alcohol concentration in order to preserve as much of the aromatic components as possible. The spirit is aged in charred American oak barrels, usually old bourbon casks, from which it gets most of its color.

Light rum is fermented with conventional yeasts and distilled industrially to about 90 percent ABV. The rum is matured to mollify its rough edges and usually filtered to remove residual color from the molasses. It is diluted to between 40 and 43 percent ABV before bottling. *Golden rums* are aged in oak barrels to mellow them further and to develop a light honey color. *Overproof rums* are diluted less before bottling and can be as high as 75 percent ABV. Premium rums that are aged for years in oak resemble brandies in appearance and flavor. Cachaça is Brazilian rum made exclusively from sugarcane juice. Charanda is sweet vanilla-tasting Mexican rum.

TEQUILA AND MESCAL

The agave, a succulent plant similar to cactus that grows at high altitudes mostly in the Jalisco state of Mexico, is the base for the indigenous liquors tequila and mescal. Both are made mostly from the hearts (piñas) of blue agave (*Agave tequilana*), which are rich in fructose and inulin (a form of indigestible long-chain sugar). Agave for tequila is steamed to break down the sugars before fermentation. Agave for mescal is roasted over charcoal, infusing the piñas with smoke that carries into the aroma of the finished spirit. The cooked piñas are mashed with water and fermented with yeast. The resulting liquid is distilled. Tequila is distilled industrially. Mescal is double distilled in small batches in pot stills made out of clay or metal.

Tequila that is bottled without any aging is called *blanco* (white) or *plata* (silver). *Oro* (gold) tequila is *blanco* tequila with added caramel coloring and flavoring to make it resemble aged tequila. *Reposado* (rested) tequila is aged for between two months and one year in oak barrels. *Añejo* (aged) tequila is aged in oak for between one and three years, and *maduro* (extra-aged) is held for more than three years.

All mescal is aged. *Blanco* or *joven* (young) mescal is aged for less than two months and is colorless. *Reposado* and *añejo* mescals are aged similarly to tequilas but in smaller barrels.

The Importance of Flavoring

Flavor is a mixture of taste and smell. Your mouth recognizes five tastes: sweet, salty, sour, bitter, and umami (savory). You are probably familiar with the first four: sweet (the taste of sugar), salty (the taste of table salt), sour (the taste of white distilled vinegar), and bitter (the taste of quinine or tonic). Umami tastes like roasted meat, aged cheese, or sautéed mushrooms.

To isolate taste from flavor, hold your nostrils closed when you eat. By eliminating aroma, all you will perceive are the five mouth tastes. In reality, taste and aroma don't live in isolation, but if you hold your nose when you take a bite of an apple, your mouth will taste sweet sugars, tart acids, and not much else. In fact, without smelling, it's difficult to tell the difference between fruits with similar textures, like apple and pear, because almost everything that "tastes" distinctive about food isn't taste at all — it's aroma.

This is largely because our noses are more sensitive than our tongues. We have about 40 million olfactory neurons picking up odors from the air and from food vapors traveling up to the nose from the back of the mouth. In comparison to the five tastes perceived on the tongue, our perception of aromas is nearly infinite and accounts for the bulk of the sensations we call "flavor."

Many ingredients, like fruits, herbs, and spices, are loaded with aromatic molecules and have strong aromas even when raw. When these flavorful ingredients are dehydrated, the aromatic molecules concentrate, making them much more powerful for tincturing alcohol.

Aroma chemicals are volatile, which means they are small enough and light enough to float through the air. Taste chemicals are larger and typically water soluble. Aroma chemicals are more similar to oils than to water, and are therefore usually fat soluble. Because of the chemical nature of alcohol, both aroma and taste molecules are partially soluble in alcohol. So when we take a sip of flavored liqueur, we are getting a concentration of flavor, with both taste and aroma molecules roiling across the palate and wafting up the back of the throat to the olfactory receptors in the nose.

Depending on the concentration of flavor molecules in an ingredient and the percentage of alcohol in the liquor being tinctured, developing a full-flavored liqueur can take anywhere from a few hours (using crushed peppercorns or grated horseradish) to several weeks (with chopped celery or pear).

The Role of Sugar

Sugar, the currency of energy for all living things, is a highly processed commodity that can take myriad forms depending on how and how much it is processed. Most sugar is derived from sugarcane, although about 30 percent of the world sugar crop comes from processed sugar beets. When you purchase a bag of white granulated sugar, it could be cane or beet sugar. Pure cane sugar is processed totally from sugarcane.

Sugarcane is very perishable and must be processed immediately after harvest, so it is produced in two stages: First it is crushed, boiled, and crystallized into unrefined raw sugar and molasses near the cane plantation, and then the raw sugar is shipped to factories for refinement. Refined sugar is sold in three forms — raw, white, and brown — and there are several products within each form.

RAW SUGAR

Raw sugar undergoes the fewest steps in processing.

* **DEMERARA SUGAR.** These large, golden, and slightly sticky crystals are taken from the first crystallization of light cane juice.

* **MUSCOVADO (BARBADOS) SUGAR.** Taken from the final crystallization of cane syrup into blackstrap molasses, the crystals are dark brown, small, strongly flavored, and sticky.

* **SUCANAT.** A trademarked raw sugar product, it is made by evaporating cane juice to create a granular rather than a crystalline texture. (The name is a contraction of "sugarcane natural.")

* **TURBINADO SUGAR.** This is demerara sugar washed of some of its molasses so it's not sticky.

* **PALM SUGAR.** Evaporated coconut palm sugar is made from the sap of the coconut palm. It is pale brown and has a mild honey-like flavor. It has a lower glycemic index than cane sugar.

* **JAGGERY.** This unrefined sugar from the Indus peninsula comes in two forms: Soft jaggery is made from palm sugar and is spreadable; sugarcane jaggery is solid and must be crushed or dissolved before it can be used.

◄ Brown sugar

◄ Maple syrup

◄ Creamy simple syrup

◄ Honey

◄ Raw sugar

◄ Agave syrup

◄ White sugar

◄ Molasses

TYPES OF WHITE SUGAR

▶ **PRESERVING SUGAR.** Large crystals (1 mm in length) made from highly refined sugar treated to dissolve easily for making jams, jellies, and preserves

▶ **GRANULATED SUGAR** (white, table). An all-purpose sugar with medium crystals (0.5 mm in length)

▶ **SUPERFINE SUGAR** (caster, ultrafine, instant dissolving, fruit, berry). Finely ground (0.1 mm in length) granulated sugar with smooth mouthfeel; dissolves without heating

▶ **CONFECTIONERS' SUGAR** (icing, powdered). Very finely crushed (0.01 mm in length) granulated sugar, mixed with about 3 percent starch to prevent clumping

▶ **CRYSTAL SUGAR** (coarse, decorating). Large crystals (2 mm in length) about four times the size of regular granulated sugar, used for decorating confections and baked goods

▶ **SANDING SUGAR.** Large, clear crystals (1 mm in length), washed with alcohol to remove dust, used for making super-clear syrups and perfectly white icings, and commonly sprinkled on cookies and doughnuts

WHITE SUGAR

Raw sugar is put through a five-step process to remove any residual color and molasses flavor.

❋ **AFFINATION.** Raw sugar is mixed with sugar syrup and centrifuged to remove any lingering bits of molasses from the surface of the crystals.

❋ **CLARIFICATION.** The cleaned sugar is heated with water to create a super-saturated solution (70 percent sucrose by weight), which is then mixed with calcium hydroxide (slaked lime) and either carbon dioxide or phosphoric acid to precipitate mineral particles that absorb microscopic impurities in the sugar and are skimmed away.

❋ **DECOLORIZATION.** The clarified syrup is filtered through activated charcoal to remove any lingering color.

❋ **CRYSTALLIZATION.** The purified syrup is heated to supersaturation, then repeatedly crystallized and vacuum-evaporated to produce white sugar.

❋ **DRYING.** The refined crystals are air-dried to produce granulated sugar that won't clump.

BROWN SUGAR

Brown sugar is not the same thing as raw sugar. It is highly refined and is made either by soaking refined white sugar in molasses syrup and recrystallizing it or by coating granulated white sugar with molasses. Light brown sugar is about 10 percent molasses, and dark brown sugar is closer to 25 percent molasses.

Because molasses contains a substantial amount of minerals and some vitamins, brown sugar is slightly more nutritious than white sugar, containing up to 2 percent minerals (mostly calcium, magnesium, iron, and potassium) and 4 percent vitamins and other materials, such as organic acids.

CARAMELIZED SUGAR

At a high enough temperature, sugar caramelizes, separating into hundreds of diverse chemicals. The colorless sweet molecule unravels, forming deep, dark pigments with a complex flavor that combines roastedness, bitterness, tartness, and sweetness accompanied by delicious aromas of butter, milk, fruit, and flowers. The more a sugar caramelizes, the more of these new flavors develop and the less sweet it tastes. See Caramelized Simple Syrup (page 24).

SIMPLE SYRUP

Granulated sugar is not completely soluble in alcohol, so it must be dissolved in water or some water-based liquid, like juice or cream, first. The standard formula is to dissolve equal parts sugar in water. The resulting syrup, known as simple syrup, can be stored in the refrigerator for months or at room temperature for several weeks; versions made with cream don't keep as long. For recipes, see next page.

Other Liquid Sweeteners

Naturally occurring liquid sugars require no precooking. They all have flavor profiles that are more aromatic than sugar, and for that reason they are usually added early on in the tincturing process to infuse their aromas into the alcohol base. Note: I never use commercial corn syrup, which is only half as sweet as sugarcane syrups and therefore waters down the liqueur too much. I also do not recommend using artificial sweeteners, which develop bitter off flavors during tincturing,

AGAVE SYRUP (AGAVE NECTAR)

Made from the boiled juices of agave cactus, agave syrup is pale golden, with a thin honey-like consistency, and is an all-natural alternative to simple syrup.

HONEY

With its bold, floral fragrance, honey can be assertive in a beverage and should only be used when its flavor is expressly desired. Unless you want a strong honey flavor, stick to pale, mild honeys, like clover and orange blossom. Honey is sweeter than sugar and should be used in a ratio of 3:4 for simple syrup.

MAPLE SYRUP

Boiling maple sap concentrates it into a syrup. In the United States, products must contain at least 2 percent pure maple syrup to be labeled "maple syrup." The highest grades of pure maple syrup tend to be taken early in the sugaring season, when the sugar content is highest and the sap is lightest in color. Lower grades are taken later, when the sap is darkest, lowest in sugar, and more bitter.

MOLASSES

Molasses is the main by-product of the production of white sugar from sugarcane and contains all of the vitamins, minerals, and flavorful micronutrients that are filtered from cane during manufacturing. It is not nearly as sweet as sugar, but it can be used to add color and richness to dark-colored liquids. The different grades of molasses (going from palest and mildest to darkest and strongest) are light, dark, and blackstrap.

MAKING SIMPLE SYRUPS

Simple syrup is truly simple to make but making a quart at a time and keeping it on hand makes it even easier to whip up a batch of fruit- or vegetable-based liqueur whenever the ingredients are in season. The first three recipes can be refrigerated for up to three months, but the creamy versions only keep for a couple of weeks.

Simple Syrup

This all-purpose simple syrup is employed in the formulas for most liqueurs.

MAKES 3 CUPS

2¼   cups water
2¼   cups granulated cane sugar

Mix the water and sugar in a small saucepan until the sugar is all moistened. Bring to a boil over medium-high heat. Stir to make sure the sugar is completely dissolved, then remove from the heat and let cool. Refrigerate for up to 3 months.

Brown Simple Syrup

Use this dark, malty simple syrup when making whiskey- and brandy-based liqueurs.

MAKES 3 CUPS

2¼   cups water
2¼   cups dark brown sugar

Mix the water and sugar in a small saucepan until the sugar is all moistened. Bring to a boil over medium-high heat. Stir to make sure the sugar is completely dissolved, then remove from the heat and let cool. Refrigerate and use within 3 months.

Caramelized Simple Syrup

I love the candy-like aromas and tastes of this sophisticated simple syrup used in tropical liqueurs and those with a brandy base.

MAKES 2 CUPS

1   cup granulated cane sugar
2   cups Simple Syrup
¼-½ cup boiling water

1. Heat the sugar in a small saucepan over medium-high heat until it begins to melt and brown at the edges. Stir with a wooden spoon. The sugar will become lumpy; keep stirring and within a few minutes it will turn a deep orange-amber and become completely fluid.

2. Stand back and carefully pour in the simple syrup. The mixture will bubble and steam violently, and the caramelized sugar in the pan will solidify.

3. Keep stirring until most of the solid caramel melts into the liquid, about 1 minute.

4. Pour through a mesh strainer into a heat-resistant measuring cup.

5. Add enough of the boiling water to make 2 cups, and stir briefly. Refrigerate in a sealed container; use within 3 months. Discard or eat the solid caramel that remains in the strainer.

Creamy Simple Syrup

Use this recipe to turn almost any liqueur creamy.

MAKES ABOUT 3 CUPS

- 1 cup heavy cream
- 1 cup granulated cane sugar
- 1 (14-ounce) can sweetened condensed milk

1. Combine the cream and sugar in a heavy saucepan. Bring to a gentle boil over medium heat, stirring frequently, especially as it approaches a boil.

2. Remove from the heat and stir in the condensed milk. Pour into a clean jar, seal, and refrigerate. Use within 2 weeks.

Tangy-Creamy Simple Syrup

This is my sweetener of choice for fruit-flavored cream liqueurs.

MAKES ABOUT 3 CUPS

- 1 cup heavy cream
- 1 cup granulated cane sugar
- 1¼ cups vanilla whole-milk yogurt, preferably Greek-style

1. Combine the cream and sugar in a heavy saucepan. Bring to a gentle boil over medium heat, stirring frequently, especially as it approaches a boil.

2. Remove from the heat and stir in the yogurt.

3. Pour into a clean jar, seal, and refrigerate; use within 2 weeks.

Brown Cow Simple Syrup

This is the perfect simple syrup for Irish Cream (page 188) and its tipsy brethren.

MAKES ABOUT 3 CUPS

- 1 cup heavy cream
- 1 cup dark brown sugar
- ¼ cup dark-roast coffee beans, coarsely cracked
- ¼ cup cacao nibs
- 1 (14-ounce) can sweetened condensed milk

1. Combine the cream, sugar, coffee, and cacao nibs in a heavy saucepan. Bring to a gentle boil over medium heat, stirring frequently, especially as the mixture approaches a boil.

2. Remove from the heat and let steep for 10 minutes.

3. Strain through a fine-mesh strainer into a clean jar, and stir in the condensed milk. Store in a sealed container in the refrigerator; use within 2 weeks.

Coconut Cream Simple Syrup

Nutty, tropical and rich, it's the perfect vehicle for a creamy dairy-free liqueur.

MAKES ABOUT 3 CUPS

- 2 (14-ounce) cans coconut milk
- 2 cups granulated cane sugar

1. Combine the coconut milk and sugar in a heavy saucepan. Bring to a gentle boil over medium heat, stirring frequently, especially as it approaches a boil.

2. Remove from the heat and cool to room temperature, stirring occasionally. Pour into a clean jar, seal, and refrigerate. Use within 2 weeks.

Simple Equipment Is All You Need

No special equipment is required for making liqueurs: A good supply of large glass jars with tight-fitting lids is the only supplement a reasonably well-appointed kitchen will need.

All but the cream liqueurs are sufficiently high in alcohol that the growth of microorganisms is nearly impossible. I don't bother sterilizing the jars I use for liqueurs; washing them with hot soapy water and rinsing thoroughly is sufficient. If that makes you uneasy, you can run your utensils and jars through the dishwasher first.

HERE'S WHAT YOU WILL NEED

* 2-quart glass measuring cup
* Digital scale
* Set of measuring spoons
* Several wooden spoons
* Whisk
* Small saucepan
* Fine-mesh strainer
* Standard-mesh strainer
* Cheesecloth
* Wide-mouth funnel
* Glass jars with lids (greater than 1-quart capacity) for tincturing
* Glass jars or bottles (1-quart capacity) for storing

Storing Your Liqueurs

You can use any bottle or jar (or cruet or decanter) with a tight-fitting lid to store your liqueurs. If you use old wine bottles or jars that contained food, make sure they are thoroughly clean. Alcohol has a tendency to lock onto and absorb residual flavors lingering in a container, which can be disastrous to delicately flavored liqueurs.

If you are using cork stoppers, use new corks, and don't use leaded crystal or flexible plastic containers. Most liqueurs (other than those with creamy additions) will keep for up to one year if tightly sealed and stored in a dark, cool place.

Simple Equipment Is All You Need

▼ 2-quart glass measuring cup

▼ Glass jars with lids

▼ Wide-mouth funnel

▼ Small saucepan

◄ Wooden spoons

◄ Digital scale

◄ Whisk

▲ Fine-mesh & standard-mesh strainers

▲ Set of measuring spoons

The Recipes

Fruit ❖ Vegetables ❖ Herbs & Spices ❖ Nuts & Seeds
Floral ❖ Coffee, Tea & Chocolate ❖ Creamy
Caramel, Syrup & Butterscotch ❖ Infused Spirits

FRUIT LIQUEURS

THERE ARE THREE WAYS TO TURN FRUIT INTO BOOZE. You can ferment it into wine, distill it into liquor, or tincture it into liqueur. The last method is not only the easiest of the three, but is also the only one that yields 100 percent true fruit flavor.

Turning fruit into wine and turning wine into liquor are complicated processes, involving hundreds of variables that precipitate delicious multilayered sensations, none of which taste like fresh fruit. In contrast, capturing the essence of fruit in liqueur is straightforward. Let's say you have a hankering for strawberries. To make strawberry liqueur, cut up a few handfuls of strawberries (with the greens or without; each will yield a different spirit), introduce the fruit to a neutral base alcohol (vodka is always good), and set the tincture aside for a few days. Within that time, the liquor will tint to the exact shade of strawberry skin, and when you pop the lid your nose will know that magic has transpired.

Those strawberries, once blushing with life, have given up their ghost to the surrounding alcohol. The berries have turned to chalk, but not for naught. The resulting liqueur has ripened, taking on the fragrance of fresh berries and a fragile tangle of sweetness and tartness. You strain away the dead strawberry carcasses and decant what nature might have intended if she had ever gone on a bender: quaffable fruit. All that's left to do is sweeten it to taste and invite over some friends.

Picking Perfect Fruit

Because the full flavor of fruit depends so much on ripeness, fresh is not always best. For any fruit whose quality is judged by that fleeting state known as "perfectly ripe," frozen or dried fruit will give you more predictable and usually better results. Frozen berries are picked at full ripeness and flash frozen, so for cooking or making liqueur they are often superior to their fresh counterparts. The flavor of dried fruit is concentrated, so you can develop a stronger flavor base with far less ingredient.

Make sure that the fruit you use is clean and unblemished. Alcohol picks up both good and bad flavors effortlessly. A little bit of mold on the edge of one piece of peach can taint a whole fifth of peach liqueur. The mold itself will not survive contact with alcohol, but its flavor will.

Preparing Your Ingredients

Because you strain out the flavoring ingredients, the preparation for most fruit liqueurs is quite simple — wash, chop, and mix with alcohol. I remove the stems from pears and apples before cutting them up but include the skins and seeds.

Thick-skinned fruit, such as melons and mangos, should be peeled and cut into small chunks. Berries can be used whole and cherries do not need to be pitted, just cut in half. Scrub citrus fruit well to remove any wax or other residue before zesting or peeling the rind.

Apple Brandy

Copycat Applejack

Homemade apple brandy, or applejack, was historically made through freeze distillation (a.k.a. jacking), a natural process of leaving barrels of hard cider outside to freeze. Because the freezing point of alcohol is lower than that of water, the frozen chunks of ice could be removed, leaving apple cider liquor. Unfortunately, freeze-distilled cider contains unwanted alcohol byproducts, like methanol and fusel alcohols, which is why applejack is now typically pot distilled.

Fortunately, when making apple liqueur from professionally distilled brandy or rum, the distillation has already been taken care of, so all you have to look for is flavor. It's delicious dousing a baked apple or drizzled over a scoop of maple walnut ice cream.

MAKES ABOUT 1 QUART

1 cup dark rum (80 proof)

2¼ cups brandy (80 proof)

4 large tart apples, such as Granny Smith, stemmed and finely chopped

1 cup Brown Simple Syrup (page 24)

1. Muddle the rum, brandy, and apples with a wooden spoon in a half-gallon jar, stirring to moisten the fruit.

2. Seal the jar and put it in a cool, dark cabinet until the liquid smells and tastes strongly of apple, about 7 days.

3. Strain the mixture with a mesh strainer into a clean quart jar. Do not push on the solids to extract more liquid.

4. Stir in the simple syrup.

5. Seal and store in a cool, dark cabinet. Use within 1 year.

Y **Cheers!** *Use in an Autumn Leaves (page 245) or a Harvest Stinger (page 253).*

Apple Spice Hooch

Think of this seductively spiced liqueur as the sippable essence of everything that makes wintertime cozy — snow falling fast, a fire snapping in the grate, and you, snugly swaddled in a throw, just finishing your last bite of pie (damn!). But as you lift your snifter of Apple Spice Hooch, you happily hum to yourself: Let it snow, let it snow, let it snow.

MAKES ABOUT 1 QUART

1 fifth (750 ml/3¼ cups)
  bourbon (80 proof)

1 cup maple syrup

4 large tart apples, such as Granny
  Smith, stemmed and finely chopped

2 cinnamon sticks, broken
  into small pieces

2 whole cloves

¼ of a whole nutmeg

1. Muddle the bourbon, maple syrup, apples, cinnamon, cloves, and nutmeg with a wooden spoon in a half-gallon jar, stirring to moisten the fruit.

2. Seal the jar and put it in a cool, dark cabinet until the liquid smells and tastes strongly of apple and cinnamon, about 7 days.

3. Strain the mixture with a mesh strainer into a clean quart jar. Do not push on the solids to extract more liquid.

4. Seal and store in a cool, dark cabinet. Use within 1 year.

Y *Santé!* *Serve warm with a cinnamon swizzle stick.*

Pure Pear

Copycat Poire William

Even if you are unfamiliar with Poire William (Williams Bon Chrétien is the name for Bartlett pears in France and most of the rest of the world), you probably have heard of its presentation. The eau-de-vie is packaged in a bottle containing a whole pear. How'd they do that?

Well, you gotta love the French. What other culture would have the Gaul (sorry) to grow fruit in a bottle? But there they are, scores of bulbous bottles dangling from Bartlett branches in the orchards of Alsace, slipped over the blossoms before they fruit to create a private greenhouse for each developing pear. This rendition is fruitier than the original. By tincturing the pear in spirits rather than distilling its juice, you develop far fuller pear flavor.

MAKES ABOUT 1 QUART

6 pears, stemmed and finely chopped

1 fifth (750 ml/3¼ cups)
   vodka (80-100 proof)

¾ cup Simple Syrup (page 24)

1. Muddle the pears with a wooden spoon in a half-gallon jar. Add the vodka, and stir to moisten the fruit.

2. Seal the jar and put it in a cool, dark cabinet until the liquid smells and tastes strongly of pear, about 7 days.

3. Strain the mixture with a mesh strainer into a clean quart jar. Do not push on the solids to extract more liquid.

4. Stir in the simple syrup.

5. Seal and store in a cool, dark cabinet. Use within 1 year.

🍸 *Salut!* *Let it bring your next vodka martini to fruition.*

Poached Pear

Pears ripen delicately; miss the peak and their flesh turns grainy, but harvest too soon and you get something closer to an apple, crisp and tart with barely any perfume. Hence the popularity of poached pears. Poaching adds sweetness and aromatics. It softens underripe crisp fibers and increases juiciness. This fragrant liqueur attempts to capture the charm of lightly poached pears without having to turn on the stove. As with all liqueurs, all you have to do is throw everything together and wait.

MAKES ABOUT 1 QUART

6 ripe pears, stemmed and finely chopped
Finely grated zest of 1 lemon
Finely grated zest of ½ orange
1 cinnamon stick, cracked
1 vanilla bean, split
2 cups vodka (80–100 proof)
2½ cups dry vermouth (18% ABV)
1 cup Simple Syrup (page 24)

1. Muddle the pears with a wooden spoon in a half-gallon jar. Add the lemon zest, orange zest, cinnamon stick, vanilla, vodka, and vermouth; stir to moisten everything.

2. Seal the jar and put it in a cool, dark cabinet until the liquid smells and tastes strongly of poached pear, about 7 days.

3. Strain the mixture with a mesh strainer into a clean quart jar. Do not push on the solids to extract more liquid.

4. Stir in the simple syrup.

5. Seal and store in a cool, dark cabinet. Use within 1 year.

Y *L'chaim!* *Serve chilled in a small wineglass.*

Always Apricot

Pronounced, à la French, ah-pree-COH, this unapologetic liqueur embodies the tangy soul of the plushest member of the drupe fruit clan (fruits with a pit). It is not complex in flavor, except for the overwhelming sensation of apricot meandering around your cranium with every sip. Its apricotiness is enhanced by the addition of almond extract, a flavor essence taken from the kernel that lies inside the pit of every drupe fruit.

MAKES ABOUT 1 QUART

1 **fifth (750 ml/3¼ cups) light rum (80 proof)**
24 **dried apricot halves, finely chopped**
1 **cup Simple Syrup (page 24)**
1 **teaspoon pure almond extract**

1. Muddle the rum and apricots with a wooden spoon in a half-gallon jar. Stir to moisten the fruit.

2. Seal the jar and put it in a cool, dark cabinet until the liquid smells and tastes strongly of apricot, 3 to 5 days.

3. Strain the mixture with a mesh strainer into a clean quart jar. Do not push on the solids to extract more liquid.

4. Stir in the simple syrup and almond extract.

5. Seal and store in a cool, dark cabinet. Use within 1 year.

Y **Bottoms Up!** *Sip as a tangy alternative to Amaretto.*

Apricardamom

This sultry liaison of cardamom and apricot will send the hedonistic soul into a swoon. The eucalyptic cardamom leaps up as lively as a Marrakech marketplace, while the lush apricot soothes like velvet. Pour yourself another shot. You're in for a helluva night.

MAKES ABOUT 1 QUART

1 **fifth (750 ml/3¼ cups) vodka (80–100 proof)**
15 **dried apricot halves, finely chopped**
20 **green cardamom pods, crushed**
1 **cup Simple Syrup (page 24)**

1. Muddle the vodka, apricots, and cardamom with a wooden spoon in a half-gallon jar. Stir to moisten everything.

2. Seal the jar and put it in a cool, dark cabinet until the liquid smells and tastes strongly of apricot and cardamom, 3 to 5 days.

3. Strain the mixture with a mesh strainer into a clean quart jar. Do not push on the solids to extract more liquid.

4. Stir in the simple syrup.

5. Seal and store in a cool, dark cabinet. Use within 1 year.

Y *Prost!* *Muddle a sprig of thyme in a highball glass, fill with ice, add 2 ounces Apricardamom, and top with ginger ale.*

Drupe Fruit Complex

Drupe fruits encompass all members of the genus Prunus, *including apricot, peach, plum, and cherry, as well as some less fruity fruits such as olive, coffee, and almond. All drupes have meaty flesh surrounding a hard-shelled pit, and all possess a lush fruitiness. This redolent fruit liqueur possesses the luxurious intensity of the group, without allowing any one specimen to dominate. In keeping with the liqueur-by-committee approach, the alcohol base is also blended — vodka for tincturing, rum for sweetness, and bourbon for pizzazz.*

MAKES ABOUT 1 QUART

1 cup vodka (80-100 proof)

1½ cups dark rum (80 proof)

1 cup bourbon (80 proof)

4 dried peach halves, chopped, or 2 ripe peaches, pitted and chopped, or 15 frozen peach slices, thawed

8 dried apricot halves, chopped, or 4 ripe apricots, pitted and chopped

3 pitted prunes, chopped, or 3 ripe plums, pitted and chopped

½ cup dried sour cherries

1 cup Simple Syrup (page 24)

1. Muddle the vodka, rum, bourbon, peaches, apricots, prunes, and cherries with a wooden spoon in a half-gallon jar. Stir to moisten everything.

2. Seal the jar and put it in a cool, dark cabinet until the liquid smells and tastes strongly of fruit, about 7 days.

3. Strain the mixture with a mesh strainer into a clean quart jar. Do not push on the solids to extract more liquid.

4. Stir in the simple syrup.

5. Seal and store in a cool, dark cabinet. Use within 1 year.

NOTE: When you drain the mixture, reserve the fruit. It is dynamite cascaded over scoops of ice cream.

. . . .

Y *Skål!* *Makes a multifaceted Manhattan with a dash of citrus bitters.*

Tropical Banana

Warm-climate tropical fruits develop a combination of fruity esters, sultry sweetness, and mild tartness that is hard to resist. That raucous combo is captured completely in this congenial, slightly creamy liqueur. The method for this mixture is a little different from that of other fruit liqueurs in the book. The fruit is muddled with sugar syrup early in processing to prevent the banana from darkening too much due to oxidation. It makes a fragrant daiquiri.

MAKES ABOUT 1 QUART

4–6 bananas, peeled and coarsely mashed (1½–2 cups)

1 mango, peeled, pitted, and chopped

1 cup Simple Syrup (page 24)

1 fifth (750 ml/3¼ cups) light rum (80 proof)

½ of a whole nutmeg

2 vanilla beans (Madagascar or Bourbon), split and broken into small pieces

1. Muddle the mashed banana, mango, and simple syrup with a wooden spoon in a half-gallon jar. Stir in the rum, nutmeg, and vanilla beans.

2. Seal the jar and put it in a cool, dark cabinet until the liquid smells and tastes strongly of banana, 2 to 4 days.

3. Strain the mixture with a mesh strainer into a clean quart jar. Do not push on the solids to extract more liquid.

4. Seal and store in a cool, dark cabinet. Use within 1 year.

Y *Sláinte!* *Try it in a Banshee (page 239).*

Blueberry Cinnamon

I am a sucker for cinnamon and blueberries; I wish I knew why. Maybe it's because I'm not much of a cinnamon freak, and I find its juxtaposition with the blueberries generates barely a hint of the Red Hots Saturday-matinee-movie sucker punch so ubiquitous in cinnamon-flavored products. This liqueur has a beautifully balanced flavor and is a gorgeous color as well.

MAKES ABOUT 1 QUART

2 pints blueberries, stemmed, or
   1½ pounds frozen blueberries, thawed
1 cup Simple Syrup (page 24)
1 fifth (750 ml/3¼ cups)
   light rum (80 proof)
4 cinnamon sticks, smashed into shards

1. Muddle the blueberries and simple syrup with a wooden spoon in a half-gallon jar. Stir in the rum and cinnamon.

2. Seal the jar and put it in a cool, dark cabinet until the liquid smells and tastes strongly of blueberries, about 7 days.

3. Strain the mixture with a mesh strainer into a clean quart jar. Do not push on the solids to extract more liquid.

4. Seal and store in a cool, dark cabinet. Use within 1 year.

Y *L'chaim!* *Drizzle over fruit cocktail.*

Blueberry Balsamic

Blueberries are saturated with antioxidants, especially in their skins, and those inflammation-relieving elements are absorbed during tincturing, making this liqueur one of the few alcoholic beverages that contains its own hangover remedy right in the bottle. The alcohol base is about one-third wine, which lowers the alcohol content and reduces its ability to capture flavorful molecules quickly. Hence it has a longer tincturing period than other fruit liqueurs.

MAKES ABOUT 1 QUART

2 pints blueberries, stemmed, or
   1½ pounds frozen blueberries, thawed

2 cups Simple Syrup (page 24)

2¼ cups vodka (80–100 proof)

1 cup fruity red wine, like Merlot
   or Cabernet Sauvignon

¼ cup aged balsamic vinegar

1. Muddle the blueberries and simple syrup with a wooden spoon in a half-gallon jar. Stir in the vodka, wine, and balsamic vinegar.

2. Seal the jar and put it in a cool, dark cabinet until the liquid smells and tastes strongly of blueberries, about 7 days.

3. Strain the mixture with a mesh strainer into a clean quart jar. Do not push on the solids to extract more liquid.

4. Seal and store in a cool, dark cabinet. Use within 1 year.

Y **Cheers!** *Sip after dinner or drizzle over fruit for an elegantly simple dessert.*

Double Raspberry

Copycat Chambord

Chambord comes in a pretentious spherical bottle caged in gold plastic and capped with a hoop crown. Its form is reminiscent of the globus cruciger, *an orb crowned with a cross that was used by medieval church-states to symbolize Christ's supremacy over the world. Illusions of grandeur for a berry liqueur, don't you think? But Chambord is no ordinary berry liqueur. The fruit is tinctured twice in Cognac and finished with honey, vanilla, and orange. My recipe is a good replica; the bottle is up to you.*

MAKES ABOUT 1 QUART

1	quart fresh red raspberries or 1½ pounds frozen raspberries, thawed
1	quart black raspberries
1	cup Simple Syrup (page 24)
½	cup honey
2	cups vodka (80-100 proof)
1¼	cups brandy (80 proof)
	Finely grated zest of ½ orange
¼	of a vanilla bean (Madagascar or Bourbon), split

1. Muddle the red and black raspberries, simple syrup, and honey with a wooden spoon in a half-gallon jar. Stir in the vodka, brandy, orange zest, and vanilla.

2. Seal the jar and put it in a cool, dark cabinet until the liquid smells and tastes strongly of raspberries, about 7 days.

3. Strain the mixture with a mesh strainer into a clean quart jar. Do not push on the solids to extract more liquid.

4. Seal and store in a cool, dark cabinet. Use within 1 year.

....

🍸 *Skål! Makes a killer Kir — try it with Champagne!*

Sweet-and-Sour Cherry

Copycat Cherry Heering

All cherries are from the drupe fruit genus (Prunus), which includes apricots, peaches, and plums. Within the genus there are two sub-categories of cherry: Sweet (or black cherries) are P. avium and sour cherries (or pie cherries) are P. cerasus. The two are no more alike than a grape and a plum.

Sweet cherries — dark or golden-skinned, meaty, and taut — are the more common in markets, largely because they are best consumed fresh. Sweet cherries have a longer growing season and greater resistance to disease than sour cherries, which are too tart to be eaten without sweetening and are somewhat loose in their skins. And yet our notion of cherry flavor — tart, tangy, and bright — is 100 percent sour cherry, as enervating and unnerving to the palate as glancing directly into the sun. This liqueur is a diplomatic blend of the two, both civilized and naughty, just the right thing to make your Singapore Sling blush.

MAKES ABOUT 1 QUART

3 cups black cherries, stemmed and crushed (no need to remove pits)

1½ cups Simple Syrup (page 24)

2 cups vodka (80–100 proof)

1½ cups brandy (80 proof)

2¼ cups dried sour cherries, coarsely chopped

1. Muddle the black cherries and simple syrup with a wooden spoon in a half-gallon jar. Stir in the vodka, brandy, and dried sour cherries.

2. Seal the jar and put it in a cool, dark cabinet until the liquid smells and tastes strongly of cherries, about 7 days.

3. Strain the mixture with a mesh strainer into a clean quart jar. Do not push on the solids to extract more liquid.

4. Seal and store in a cool, dark cabinet. Use within 1 year.

Y *Sláinte!* Make a Bittersweet Sour Cherry (page 246).

Cherry Vanilla

Like puppies dressed in pants and kittens wearing bonnets, the combination of cherry and vanilla has "Awww" power — it's just so cute and sweet and kind of cuddly. This is a scrumptious liqueur, so overtly fruity and fragrant that you could down a quart without noticing that you have done anything untoward. Pour it over ice, drizzle it over ice cream, or use it in an ice cream soda served with two straws and just say, "Awww!"

MAKES ABOUT 1 QUART

1 fifth (750 ml/3¼ cups) vodka (80-100 proof)

2 pints sour cherries, stemmed and crushed (no need to remove pits), or 2½ cups dried sour cherries, coarsely chopped

2 vanilla beans (Madagascar or Bourbon), split

1 cup Simple Syrup (page 24)

1. Muddle the vodka, cherries, and vanilla with a wooden spoon in a half-gallon jar. Stir to moisten everything.

2. Seal the jar and put it in a cool, dark cabinet until the liquid smells and tastes strongly of cherries — 3 to 5 days for dried fruit, about 7 days for fresh fruit.

3. Strain the mixture with a mesh strainer into a clean quart jar. Do not push on the solids to extract more liquid.

4. Stir in the simple syrup.

5. Seal and store in a cool, dark cabinet. Use within 1 year.

Y *Cheers!* *Serve 2 ounces in a tall glass with a scoop of ice cream and seltzer.*

In Praise of Fraise

You're walking through a field of grass dotted with wild strawberries. The ground is damp and uneven, a shifting carpet. You try not to tread on the treasured fruit, but every now and then you miscalculate, creating an invisible cloud of strawberry-scented air, and you thank the gods who grace us with gifts for our clumsiness. This liqueur is single-minded: It thinks of nothing but ripe strawberries, and in its simplistic innocence it sings sweetly.

MAKES ABOUT 1 QUART

2 pints strawberries, hulled and sliced, or 1½ pounds frozen strawberries, thawed

1½ cups Simple Syrup (page 24)

1 fifth (750 ml/3¼ cups) vodka (80–100 proof)

1. Muddle the strawberries and simple syrup with a wooden spoon in a half-gallon jar. Stir in the vodka.

2. Seal the jar and put it in a cool, dark cabinet until the liquid smells and tastes strongly of strawberries, about 7 days.

3. Strain the mixture with a mesh strainer into a clean quart jar. Do not push on the solids to extract more liquid.

4. Seal and store in a cool, dark cabinet. Use within 1 year.

Y *Santé!* *Perfect for sipping on a summer day, for spiking a Cosmo, for dabbing behind each ear.*

Strawberry Tart

Ripeness is misunderstood. We tend to think of it as either the presence of sweetness or the absence of tartness, when in reality perfect ripeness contains the perfect balance between the two. Underripe is too tart and overripe is too sweet, even slightly rotten-tasting, but ripeness is just right. Because liqueurs are sweetened, it is easy to err on the rotted side. Adding a bit of fruit vinegar to that sweet elixir restores the balance.

MAKES ABOUT 1 QUART

2 pints strawberries, hulled and sliced, or 1½ pounds frozen strawberries, thawed

1½ cups Simple Syrup (page 24)

1 fifth (750 ml/3¼ cups) vodka (80-100 proof)

1 tablespoon strawberry or raspberry vinegar

1. Muddle the strawberries and simple syrup with a wooden spoon in a half-gallon jar. Stir in the vodka.

2. Seal the jar and put it in a cool, dark cabinet until the liquid smells and tastes strongly of strawberries, about 7 days.

3. Strain the mixture with a mesh strainer into a clean quart jar. Do not push on the solids to extract more liquid.

4. Stir in the vinegar.

5. Seal and store in a cool, dark cabinet. Use within 1 year.

Y *Bottoms Up!* *Serve in a tall glass with lemon and lots of ice.*

Strawberry-Rhubarb Twin Tamer

Strawberry and rhubarb are mismatched twins, stuck in the same culinary pram because of their sweet-tart affinity but suffering from boundary issues whenever they are conjoined on the stove. The two cook at wildly different rates, so in recipes that call for simmering the two together, the strawberries inevitably overcook while the rhubarb stays stubbornly crunchy. The obvious solution is to eliminate all texture issues and make liqueur.

MAKES ABOUT 1 QUART

2 pints strawberries, hulled and sliced, or 1½ pounds frozen strawberries, thawed

3 stalks rhubarb, chopped, or 10 ounces frozen rhubarb, thawed

2 cups Simple Syrup (page 24)

1 fifth (750 ml/3¼ cups) light rum (80 proof)

1. Muddle the strawberries, rhubarb, and simple syrup with a wooden spoon in a half-gallon jar. Stir in the rum.

2. Seal the jar and put it in a cool, dark cabinet until the liquid smells and tastes strongly of strawberries and rhubarb, about 7 days.

3. Strain the mixture with a mesh strainer into a clean quart jar. Do not push on the solids to extract more liquid.

4. Seal and store in a cool, dark cabinet. Use within 1 year.

Y *Prost!* *Use to spike lemonade or any fruit punch.*

Cranberry Clarity

Like Roto-Rooter for your head, this drinkable Dremel boosts the pucker of cranberries with a sinus-swabbing blast of horseradish. Don't let its pretty garnet-tinted glint fool you. This is a powerful concoction. Serve it with orange or grapefruit juice, or simply with a splash of soda when you need to power-wash the old brainstem.

MAKES ABOUT 1 QUART

1 **pound fresh or frozen cranberries, crushed**
1 **cup Simple Syrup (page 24)**
1 **fifth (750 ml/3¼ cups) vodka (80-100 proof)**
1 **(3-inch) piece fresh horseradish root, peeled and coarsely shredded**

1. Muddle the cranberries and simple syrup with a wooden spoon in a half-gallon jar. Stir in the vodka.

2. Seal the jar and put it in a cool, dark cabinet until the liquid smells and tastes strongly of fruit, about 3 days. Add the horseradish.

3. Seal the jar and set aside until the liquid smells strongly of horseradish, about 1 day.

4. Strain the mixture with a mesh strainer into a clean quart jar. Do not push on the solids to extract more liquid.

5. Seal and store in a cool, dark cabinet. Use within 1 year.

Y *Santé!* *Make a Madras Cocktail (page 244) — good for what ails you!*

Pure Cranberry

Similar to sour cherries, raw cranberries are packed with flavor that needs sugar to become accessible. To make cranberry sauce or a cherry pie, the fruit is usually macerated with sugar and cooked to make it palatable. Here the process is simpler: Mix the raw berries with sugar syrup, add a fifth of booze, and let time work some magic. The result refracts light like a ruby and bounces about your palate like a Hacky Sack on the heels of an agile teen.

MAKES ABOUT 1 QUART

1 **pound fresh or frozen cranberries, crushed**

1 **cup Simple Syrup (page 24)**

1 **fifth (750 ml/3¼ cups) vodka (80–100 proof)**

1. Muddle the cranberries and simple syrup with a wooden spoon in a half-gallon jar. Stir in the vodka.

2. Seal the jar and put it in a cool, dark cabinet until the liquid smells and tastes strongly of fruit, about 7 days.

3. Strain the mixture with a mesh strainer into a clean quart jar. Do not push on the solids to extract more liquid.

4. Seal and store in a cool, dark cabinet. Use within 1 year.

Y *Santé! Makes a stellar Cosmo.*

Melba Blush

Nellie Melba, the once world-renowned prima donna of the Paris and Metropolitan operas, is now better known for lending her name to the popular dessert. The luscious combination of peaches and strawberries was created at the Savoy Hotel in London by Georges Auguste Escoffier, the famous French chef, who served it over ice cream in honor of Mme Melba. The flavor struck a chord with the dining public, and this fragrant liqueur will remind you why. It has a glorious pale-salmon tint and a delicious richness.

MAKES ABOUT 1 QUART

1　pint fresh raspberries, or
　　12 ounces frozen raspberries
1　cup Simple Syrup (page 24)
6　dried peach halves, finely chopped,
　　or 3 fresh peaches, pitted and
　　finely chopped, or 20 frozen
　　peach slices, thawed
2¼　cups vodka (80–100 proof)
1　cup light rum (80 proof)

1. Muddle the raspberries and simple syrup with a wooden spoon in a half-gallon jar. Stir in the peaches, vodka, and rum.

2. Seal the jar and put it in a cool, dark cabinet until the liquid smells and tastes strongly of raspberries and peaches, about 7 days.

3. Strain the mixture with a mesh strainer into a clean quart jar. Do not push on the solids to extract more liquid.

4. Seal and store in a cool, dark cabinet. Use within 1 year.

Y *Sláinte!* *Sip after dinner or drizzle over ice cream.*

La Pêche

Copycat Peach Schnapps

Peach fragrance is fleeting, which is why peach perfume captured in an imbibable form tastes radically magical. Herbal dry vermouth is added after tincturing to enhance the floral quality of peach. Although you could put everything together all at once, starting out with a high concentration of alcohol speeds up the transfer of fruit flavor into the liquid.

MAKES ABOUT 1 QUART

1⅓ cups vodka (90 proof)

12 dried peach halves, finely chopped, or 5 fresh peaches, pitted and finely chopped, or 30 frozen peach slices, thawed

1¼ cups dry vermouth (18% ABV)

1 cup Simple Syrup (page 24)

1. Muddle the vodka and peaches with a wooden spoon in a half-gallon jar. Stir to moisten the fruit.

2. Seal the jar and put it in a cool, dark cabinet until the liquid smells and tastes strongly of peach — 3 to 5 days if using dried fruit, about 7 days for fresh fruit.

3. Strain the mixture with a mesh strainer into a clean quart jar. Do not push on the solids to extract more liquid.

4. Stir in the vermouth and simple syrup.

5. Seal and store in a cool, dark cabinet. Use within 1 year.

🍸 *L'chaim!* *Mix with Champagne for an easy Bellini.*

Ginger-Peach Sake

Genshu is undiluted sake (Murai is a popular brand). With half the proof of distilled liquors, genshu has a similar alcohol concentration to vermouth and is best supplemented with vodka to ensure sufficient alcohol for tincturing. Because of its slightly reduced alcohol concentration, this liqueur needs to cure for more than a week to build full flavor. The ginger tinctures faster than the peach, so I have purposely kept the amount of ginger small. If you want more zip, feel free to use a 2-inch piece of fresh ginger.

MAKES ABOUT 1 QUART

1½ cups genshu sake (18 to 20% ABV)
2 cups vodka, preferably rice vodka, like Kai (80 proof)
12 dried peach halves, chopped
1 (1-inch) piece fresh ginger, coarsely shredded
1 cup Simple Syrup (page 24)

1. Muddle the sake, vodka, peaches, and ginger with a wooden spoon in a half-gallon jar. Stir to moisten everything.

2. Seal the jar and put it in a cool, dark cabinet until the liquid smells and tastes strongly of ginger and peach, 7 to 10 days.

3. Strain the mixture with a mesh strainer into a clean quart jar. Do not push on the solids to extract more liquid.

4. Stir in the simple syrup.

5. Seal and store in a cool, dark cabinet. Use within 1 year.

Y *Prost!* *Serve well chilled by the shot.*

Peach Pit

Peaches have an affinity for almonds, which is only fitting, since they come from the same family tree. Well, almost the same: Peaches and almonds are botanical cousins. Almond fruit looks like a small leathery peach, and inside every peach pit is a seed that looks and tastes like a bitter almond. In this liqueur, I've reinforced the connection by adding a hint of almond extract.

MAKES ABOUT 1 QUART

1 fifth (750 ml/3¼ cups) vodka (80-100 proof)

12 dried peach halves, finely chopped, or 5 fresh peaches, pitted and finely chopped, or 30 frozen peach slices, thawed

1 cup Simple Syrup (page 24)

⅛ teaspoon pure almond extract

1. Muddle the vodka and peaches with a wooden spoon in a half-gallon jar. Stir to moisten the fruit.

2. Seal the jar and put it in a cool, dark cabinet until the liquid smells and tastes strongly of peaches — 3 to 5 days if using dried fruit, about 7 days for fresh fruit.

3. Strain the mixture with a mesh strainer into a clean quart jar. Do not push on the solids to extract more liquid.

4. Stir in the simple syrup and almond extract.

5. Seal and store in a cool, dark cabinet. Use within 1 year.

Y *Bottoms Up!* *You can sip this straight up, but it tastes amazing drizzled over butter almond ice cream.*

Fruity Wine Liqueur

Wine is fermented grape juice. Obviously it needs to be sweetened to turn it toward liqueur, but here we up the flavor ante by reinforcing it with crushed grapes and adding a hefty dose of brandy to pump up the alcohol and lend an oaky hint of vanilla.

MAKES ABOUT 1 QUART

2 pounds red grapes, preferably with seeds, crushed

1 cup Simple Syrup (page 24)

1 cup fruity red wine, like Merlot

2 cups brandy (80 proof)

1. Muddle the grapes and simple syrup with a wooden spoon in a half-gallon jar. Stir in the red wine and brandy.

2. Seal the jar and put it in a cool, dark cabinet until the liquid smells and tastes strongly of fruit, about 7 days.

3. Strain the mixture with a mesh strainer into a clean jar. Do not push on the solids to extract more liquid.

4. Seal and store in a cool, dark cabinet. Use within 1 year.

🍸 *Skål!* Sip this liqueur straight, or warm it gently in a big-bowled snifter rotated lazily above a candle flame.

Clear Orange

Copycat Triple Sec

Triple sec is a bitter-orange liqueur similar to Curaçao (which is often tinted blue), and achieves its rounded profile from the combo of bitter and sweet orange peel. The fragrant oils in the peel give triple sec its orange blossom perfume, but they also bond with the alcohol, lending a rich, fatty mouthfeel to this crystal-clear elixir. Use it for Mimosas, Boxcars, and Margaritas.

MAKES ABOUT 1 QUART

1 **fifth (750 ml/3¼ cups) vodka (80–100 proof)**
   Finely grated zest of 8 oranges
2 **tablespoons dried bitter orange peel**
1 **cup Simple Syrup (page 24)**

1. Muddle the vodka, orange zest, and dried orange peel with a wooden spoon in a half-gallon jar. Stir to moisten everything.

2. Seal the jar and put it in a cool, dark cabinet until the liquid smells and tastes strongly of orange, 5 to 7 days.

3. Strain the mixture with a mesh strainer into a clean quart jar. Do not push on the solids to extract more liquid.

4. Stir in the simple syrup.

5. Seal and store in a cool, dark cabinet. Use within 1 year.

Y *Cheers!* *Try a L'Orange (page 252) or a Streamlined Margarita (page 252).*

Orange Brandy

Copycat Grand Marnier

Triple sec and Grand Marnier are both orange flavored, but that's where the similarity ends. Grand Marnier is cognac-based, brown, richer in flavor, and more savory — an oaky, caramelized gentlemen's club drink. Triple sec is a sweeter citrus white spirit. That said, they have similar functions. Both are used extensively in cooking, and either one can spark up a Margarita, a Cosmo, or a Mimosa.

MAKES ABOUT 1 QUART

1 fifth (750 ml/3¼ cups) brandy,
   preferably cognac (80 proof)
   Finely grated zest of 8 oranges
2 tablespoons dried bitter orange peel
1 cup Brown Simple Syrup (page 25)

1. Muddle the brandy, orange zest, and dried orange peel with a wooden spoon in a half-gallon jar. Stir to moisten everything.

2. Seal the jar and put it in a cool, dark cabinet until the liquid smells and tastes strongly of orange, 3 to 5 days.

3. Strain the mixture with a mesh strainer into a clean quart jar. Do not push on the solids to extract more liquid.

4. Stir in the simple syrup.

5. Seal and store in a cool, dark cabinet. Use within 1 year.

Y *L'chaim!* *Make batches of Clear Orange and Orange Brandy and conduct your own taste test.*

Lemon Drop

Copycat Limoncello

Overtly candied and sunshine yellow, this is liquefied lemon drops — that hard, tart, mouth-slicking movie candy — and like its progenitor, it is wildly addictive. It is also a type of limoncello, although I find it fresher tasting, more aromatic, and less cloying than most limoncello I have encountered. I attribute that to the short tincturing time.

In the Old World, fruit liqueurs were often set aside to flavor for months rather than days. I'm not sure what they were trying to achieve, but curing fruit for that long in alcohol wipes out all of its subtlety. The aromatics dissipate and bitter tannins and aldehydes take over. Most fruit liqueurs hit their flavor apex after somewhere around a week of tincturing; after that the returns diminish with every passing day.

MAKES ABOUT 1 QUART

1½ cups vodka (80–100 proof)
1 cup dry vermouth (18% ABV)
Finely grated zest of 10 lemons
1 cup Simple Syrup (page 24)

1. Muddle the vodka, vermouth, and lemon zest with a wooden spoon in a half-gallon jar. Stir to moisten the zest.

2. Seal the jar and put it in a cool, dark cabinet until the liquid smells and tastes strongly of lemon, about 7 days.

3. Strain the mixture with a mesh strainer into a clean quart jar. Do not push on the solids to extract more liquid.

4. Stir in the simple syrup.

5. Seal and store in a cool, dark cabinet. Use within 1 year.

Y **Santé!** *Sip icy cold on its own as pictured or try a Lemon Tree (page 244).*

Lemon Lime

To achieve the sparkling acidic brightness of lemon-lime soda, you need to add a little citric acid (the acid in vitamin C). It would be nice to be able to use citrus juice, but it doesn't work. Its volatile flavors dissipate too quickly, and to achieve the right acid balance you would need to add so much juice that the alcohol content would drop too low to tincture. Citric acid is available in most markets and some pharmacies; it is sometimes labeled "sour salt."

MAKES ABOUT 1 QUART

1 fifth (750 ml/3¼ cups)
   vodka (80-100 proof)
   Finely grated zest of 5 lemons
   Finely grated zest of 5 limes
1 teaspoon citric acid
1 cup Simple Syrup (page 24)

1. Muddle the vodka, lemon zest, and lime zest with a wooden spoon in a half-gallon jar. Stir to moisten the zests.

2. Seal the jar and put it in a cool, dark cabinet until the liquid smells and tastes strongly of citrus, about 7 days.

3. Stir in the citric acid. Wait for 5 minutes. Strain the mixture with a mesh strainer into a clean quart jar. Do not push on the solids to extract more liquid.

4. Stir in the simple syrup.

5. Seal and store in a cool, dark cabinet. Use within 1 year.

⠀⠀⠀⠀⠀

Y **Bottoms Up!** *Use in any Sour recipe.*

Lime Agave

Infuse a bottle of tequila with a flock of limes and a slurp of agave cactus sweetener and your Margarita is as good as made. All you need is a glass of ice and a dash of Clear Orange (page 58). Agave syrup is available in most grocery stores.

MAKES ABOUT 1 QUART

1 fifth (750 ml/3¼ cups) reposado tequila (80 proof)

Finely grated zest of 10 limes

1 cup agave syrup

1. Muddle the tequila and lime zest with a wooden spoon in a half-gallon jar. Stir to moisten the zest.

2. Seal the jar and put it in a cool, dark cabinet until the liquid smells and tastes strongly of lime, about 7 days.

3. Strain the mixture with a mesh strainer into a clean quart jar. Do not push on the solids to extract more liquid.

4. Stir in the agave syrup.

5. Seal and store in a cool, dark cabinet. Use within 1 year.

🍸 *Salut!* *Try this versatile liqueur in a Bloody Maria (page 241), Streamlined Margarita (page 252), or Tequila and Tonic (page 256).*

Honeyed Grapefruit

When I was growing up, grapefruit were sadistically bitter, and on Sunday mornings it was common practice to gild your open-faced serving with a slather of honey or a knoll of white sugar. Over the decades, however, grapefruit has been reengineered to become the epitome of clean, sophisticated, sweet-tart citrus flavor. Though additional sweetener is no longer necessary, I become nostalgic for the mingled flavors of honey and grapefruit — whenever I taste one, my tongue papillae stand up and look around for the other.

MAKES ABOUT 1 QUART

1 **fifth (750 ml/3¼ cups) vodka (80–100 proof)**
   Finely grated zest of 4 grapefruits
1 **cup honey**

1. Muddle the vodka, grapefruit zest, and honey with a wooden spoon in a half-gallon jar. Stir to moisten the zest.

2. Seal the jar and put it in a cool, dark cabinet until the liquid smells and tastes strongly of grapefruit, about 7 days.

3. Strain the mixture with a mesh strainer into a clean quart jar. Do not push on the solids to extract more liquid.

4. Seal and store in a cool, dark cabinet. Use within 1 year.

Y *Prost!* *Blend with Campari over ice or use in place of vermouth for a dashing Martini.*

Grapefruit Tonic

The pith of citrus is naturally bitter (an effect from potent anti-oxidants in the peel called aldehydes), although this nutritious off flavor has been largely bred out of most citrus, except for grapefruit. This liqueur ups the bitter component by teaming grapefruit with cinchona, the tropical bark that provides quinine, the flavoring for tonic water. Long known as a strong anti-inflammatory medication, quinine was the first treatment for malaria. By infusing the cinchona and grapefruit into gin, you only need to add a splash of soda for an instant citrus-laced Gin and Tonic. Cinchona is available online in bark and powdered form (see Resources, page 257).

MAKES ABOUT 1 QUART

1 fifth (750 ml/3¼ cups) English-style gin (80 proof)
Finely grated zest of 4 grapefruits
1 cup cinchona bark pieces
1½ cups Simple Syrup (page 24)

1. Muddle the vodka, grapefruit zest, cinchona bark, and simple syrup with a wooden spoon in a half-gallon jar. Stir to moisten everything.

2. Seal the jar and put it in a cool, dark cabinet until the liquid smells and tastes strongly of grapefruit, about 10 days.

3. Strain the mixture with a mesh strainer into a clean quart jar. Do not push on the solids to extract more liquid.

4. Stir in the simple syrup.

5. Seal and store in a cool, dark cabinet. Use within 1 year.

Y *Skål! Use in Tequila and Tonic (page 256).*

Persimmon Sunrise

Persimmons come in astringent and non-astringent varieties. For liqueurs you want to stick to the non-astringent type, and the most popular varietal is Fuyu. Fuyu persimmons are bright orange and round, tapering at one end. They are sweet even when not super soft, but they have the best flavor and make the best liqueur when fully ripe and soft. A slight cracking in the skin is an indication of ripeness. This colorful and fragrant liqueur is tinted and acidified with a handful of fresh cranberries.

MAKES ABOUT 1 QUART

1 fifth (750 ml/3¼ cups) reposado
   tequila (80 proof)
3 Fuyu persimmons, trimmed
   and finely chopped
1 cup fresh cranberries, chopped
   Finely grated zest of 1 orange
1 cup Simple Syrup (page 24)

1. Muddle the tequila, persimmons, cranberries, and orange zest with a wooden spoon in a half-gallon jar. Stir to moisten everything.

2. Seal the jar and put it in a cool, dark cabinet until the liquid smells and tastes strongly of persimmon, about 10 days.

3. Strain the mixture with a mesh strainer into a clean quart jar. Do not push on the solids to extract more liquid.

4. Stir in the simple syrup.

5. Seal and store in a cool, dark cabinet. Use within 1 year.

Y *L'chaim!* *Makes an all-natural Tequila Sunrise.*

Pom-Pom

In the Northern Hemisphere, pomegranate is a winter fruit, appearing in early October and gone by the middle of February. Because it is so stubbornly seasonal, it makes sense to capture its essence for imbibing year-round. It is one of the easiest fruits to tincture because it is loaded with juice. I use just the seeds, although I have seen recipes for tincturing the whole fruit. Doing so yields a little more astringency but also darkens the color substantially, because the white pith tends to oxidize.

MAKES ABOUT 1 QUART

1 fifth (750 ml/3¼ cups)
   vodka (80–100 proof)
   Seeds from 3 pomegranates
1 cup Simple Syrup (page 24)

1. Muddle the vodka and pomegranate seeds with a wooden spoon in a half-gallon jar.

2. Seal the jar and put it in a cool, dark cabinet until the liquid smells and tastes strongly of pomegranate, 3 to 5 days.

3. Strain the mixture with a mesh strainer into a clean quart jar. Do not push on the solids to extract more liquid.

4. Stir in the simple syrup.

5. Seal and store in a cool, dark cabinet. Use within 1 year.

🍸 *Santé!* *Mix with gin for a fragrant Martini, make a cardinal-red Pomegranate Negroni (page 254) or try a Hawaiian Punch (page 244) or Coconut Mai Tai (page 250).*

Summer Cantaloupe

The musky perfume of cantaloupe can be overwhelming, which is why I prefer to imbibe my muskmelon rather than eat it out of hand. An acrid bite of alcohol and a little hint of citrus are all you need to clean up the feral notes that a ripe cantaloupe can impart.

MAKES ABOUT 1 QUART

1 fifth (750 ml/3¼ cups)
   vodka (80-100 proof)
4 cups cantaloupe chunks
   Finely grated zest of 2 lemons
1 cup Simple Syrup (page 24)

1. Muddle the vodka, cantaloupe, and lemon zest with a wooden spoon in a half-gallon jar. Stir to moisten everything.

2. Seal the jar and put it in a cool, dark cabinet until the liquid smells and tastes strongly of melon, 4 to 7 days.

3. Strain the mixture with a mesh strainer into a clean quart jar. Do not push on the solids to extract more liquid.

4. Stir in the simple syrup.

5. Seal and store in a cool, dark cabinet. Use within 1 year.

Y *Sláinte!* *Pairs nicely with summer gin coolers, white wine spritzers, and frozen Daiquiris.*

Minty Melon

The demise of the ripe honeydew melon is one of the saddest things in the annals of contemporary produce. At one time, the fresh, barely yielding flesh of a newly cleaved honeydew was the very essence of summer. Now I am told to age my cucumber-crisp specimen until it "ripens," but melons do not ripen off the vine, and since they can't be cooked and they make dismal preserves, the best thing to do is whip up a batch of melon liqueur. Because you are adding sugar, the sweetness of the melon is immaterial, and because the flesh will be discarded, its hardness hardly matters. And what you achieve is redemption from the past, as once again the regal honeydew mounts its summertime throne.

MAKES ABOUT 1 QUART

1 fifth (750 ml/3¼ cups) vodka
   (80-100 proof)
4 cups honeydew chunks
½ cup chopped fresh mint leaves
1 cup Simple Syrup (page 24)

1. Muddle the vodka, honeydew, and mint with a wooden spoon in a half-gallon jar. Stir to moisten everything.

2. Seal the jar and put it in a cool, dark cabinet until the liquid smells and tastes strongly of melon and mint, about 7 days.

3. Strain the mixture with a mesh strainer into a clean quart jar. Do not push on the solids to extract more liquid.

4. Stir in the simple syrup.

5. Seal and store in a cool, dark cabinet. Use within 1 year.

Y **Cheers!** *Toast the season with an End-of-Summer Cocktail (page 243).*

Coconut Date

The fruit of two types of palm sway together in this fragrant, slightly creamy tropical liqueur. Shards of nut and fruit are infused into rum and then sweetened with caramelized sugar to create a brandy-like elixir.

MAKES ABOUT 3 CUPS

1 fifth (750 ml/3¼ cups)
  light rum (80 proof)
3 cups lightly packed sweetened
  flaked coconut
24 Medjool dates, pitted and chopped
½ cup Caramelized Simple
  Syrup (page 24)

1. Muddle the rum, coconut, and dates with a wooden spoon in a half-gallon jar. Stir to moisten everything.

2. Seal the jar and put it in a cool, dark cabinet until the liquid smells and tastes strongly of coconut, about 10 days.

3. Strain the mixture with a mesh strainer into a clean quart jar. Do not push on the solids to extract more liquid.

4. Stir in the simple syrup.

5. Seal and store in a cool, dark cabinet. Use within 1 year.

....

Y *Bottoms Up!* *Pour over crushed ice for an instant Daiquiri or mix up a twist on a Coconut Mai Tai (page 250).*

Fragrant Fig Mead

Mead is the ancient wine made by fermenting honey. When fruit is added to the fermentation, mead technically becomes melomel, and when you mix in spices it is called metheglin. Neither term trips off my tongue as easily as mead, so I choose poetry over accuracy in titling this recipe. And rightly so, for the choreography of this fragrant chai-spiced honey-and-fig quintessence is more poetical than corporeal. It is a drink so perfectly balanced and self-contained that I suggest you prepare it frequently and sip it happily unadorned.

MAKES ABOUT 1 QUART

1	cup water
3	chai tea bags
1½	cups honey
1	fifth (750 ml/3¼ cups) brandy (80 proof)
24	dried Turkish figs, chopped

1. Bring the water to a boil. Add the tea bags, remove from the heat, and set aside for 3 minutes. Remove the tea bags and stir in the honey until it dissolves. Let cool completely.

2. Mix the honey mixture, brandy, and figs in a half-gallon jar. Stir to moisten the fruit.

3. Seal the jar and put it in a cool, dark cabinet until the liquid smells and tastes strongly of aromatic spices and figs, 2 to 3 days.

4. Strain the mixture with a mesh strainer into a clean quart jar. Do not push on the solids to extract more liquid.

5. Seal and store in a cool, dark cabinet. Use within 1 year.

Y *Salut!* *Mix up a Harvest Stinger (page 253).*

Prunelle

Copycat Plum Brandy

Some dried fruits are readily identifiable as descendants of their fresh forebears. Dried peaches aren't unlike peaches. One can see that a dried apricot came from the fresh fruit of the same name. But others don't seem to relate at all. Raisins bear little resemblance to grapes, and prunes have as much to do with plums as a beefsteak tomato has to do with a beef steak (at least the latter two complement one another on a plate). And yet plum-flavored liqueurs can be made most deliciously from prunes. This one is a classic pairing of prunes and brandy, with a hint of orange.

MAKES ABOUT 1 QUART

1¼ cups vodka (80-100 proof)
2¼ cups brandy (80 proof)
24 pitted prunes, chopped
   Finely grated zest of 1 orange
1 cup Simple Syrup (page 24)

1. Combine the vodka, brandy, prunes, and orange zest in a half-gallon jar. Stir to moisten everything.

2. Seal the jar and put it in a cool, dark cabinet until the liquid smells and tastes strongly of prunes, about 7 days.

3. Strain the mixture with a mesh strainer into a clean quart jar. Do not push on the solids to extract more liquid.

4. Stir in the simple syrup.

5. Seal and store in a cool, dark cabinet. Use within 1 year.

🍸 **Prost!** *Make a Sloe Gin Fizz (page 255), Elk (page 248), or Prunelle Martini (page 248).*

Dark and Stormy Pineapple

Embrace the dark side of pineapple. I can relate to the light, bright, tropical-romp aspect of pineapple, all Piña Coladas and paper parasols, but I'm also partial to the big boy's sultry side — the one that goes with baked ham, luaus, and upside-down everything. That's the laid-back dude I'm honoring by mixing my pineapple liqueur with dark rum, cloves, and brown sugar syrup.

MAKES ABOUT 1 QUART

1   fifth (750 ml/3¼ cups)
    dark rum (80 proof)
3   cups crushed pineapple
2   whole cloves
1½ cups Brown Simple Syrup (page 24)

1. Muddle the rum, pineapple, and cloves with a wooden spoon in a half-gallon jar. Stir to moisten everything.

2. Seal the jar and put it in a cool, dark cabinet until the liquid smells and tastes strongly of pineapple, 3 to 5 days.

3. Strain the mixture with a mesh strainer into a clean quart jar. Do not push on the solids to extract more liquid.

4. Stir in the simple syrup.

5. Seal and store in a cool, dark cabinet. Use within 1 year.

Y *Skål! The perfect spike for rum punches, Mai Tais (Coconut Mai Tai, page 250), or a New-Fashioned Old-Fashioned (page 249).*

Kiwi Lime

Like many exotic fruits, kiwi has a tutti-frutti personality — grape, citrus, honeydew, and pineapple all genomed into one adorable little package. With its fuzzy-wuzzy skin, vegetable-green flesh, and graphic ring of onyx-black seeds, it's a visual knockout, too, and all of that oddity emerges brilliantly in this liqueur. Amended with lime zest and a scant amount of sugar, this large berry's complicated nuances come through loud and clear. There is nothing like this liqueur made commercially, but I can attest that it makes a stellar Daiquiri. Or you can pour it directly over ice for an instant Caipiroska.

MAKES ABOUT 1 QUART

1 fifth (750 ml/3¼ cups) vodka
  (80-100 proof)
5 kiwis, peeled and finely chopped
  Finely grated zest of 2 limes
1 cup Simple Syrup (page 24)

1. Combine the vodka, kiwis, lime zest, and simple syrup in a half-gallon jar. Stir to moisten everything.

2. Seal the jar and put it in a cool, dark cabinet until the liquid smells and tastes strongly of kiwi, about 7 days.

3. Strain the mixture with a mesh strainer into a clean quart jar. Do not push on the solids to extract more liquid.

4. Seal and store in a cool, dark cabinet. Use within 1 year.

Y **Sláinte!** *Try a Kiwi Flower Crush (page 250).*

Mango Twist

The sheer sensual fleshiness of ripe mango is so stunning that it is surprising how much flavor you notice when that flesh actually vanishes, which is exactly what happens in this tropical breeze of a liqueur. The mangoes release all of their lush fruit flavor directly into the rum. Use this liqueur instead of triple sec in your Margaritas. Pour it over rocks, spiked with a shake of jalapeño hot sauce, or blend it with coconut ice cream, rum, and ice for a dairy-free smoothie.

MAKES ABOUT 1 QUART

1 fifth (750 ml/3¼ cups) dark rum (80 proof)

3 very ripe mangoes, pitted and finely chopped

Grated zest of 2 limes

Grated zest of 1 lemon

1 cup Simple Syrup (page 24)

1. Muddle the rum, mangoes, and both zests with a wooden spoon in a half-gallon jar. Stir to moisten everything.

2. Seal the jar and put it in a cool, dark cabinet until the liquid smells and tastes strongly of mango, 3 to 5 days.

3. Strain the mixture with a mesh strainer into a clean quart jar. Do not push on the solids to extract more liquid.

4. Stir in the simple syrup.

5. Seal and store in a cool, dark cabinet. Use within 1 year.

Y **Cheers!** *Makes a terrific Mango Martini (page 248).*

Mangocello

The Italians make deceptively lethal digestifs known as spaccafegati (translates as "liver splitters") by tincturing fruit in pure ethyl alcohol (190 proof) diluted with sugar syrup. The most famous spaccafegato is limoncello, and this orange-mango liqueur is its tropical offspring. I blend the fruit with a less deadly combo of vodka and golden rum, which bolsters the floral fragrance of mango with the caramelized sweetness of rum, and requires far less added sugar than when using pure alcohol. Serve Mangocello very cold in well-chilled shot glasses.

MAKES ABOUT 1 QUART

2 cups vodka (80–100 proof)

2 cups golden rum (80 proof)

4 very ripe mangoes, pitted and finely chopped

Grated zest of 3 large oranges

1 cup Caramelized Simple Syrup (page 24)

1. Combine the vodka, rum, mangoes, and orange zest in a half-gallon jar. Stir to moisten everything.

2. Seal the jar and put it in a cool, dark cabinet until the liquid smells and tastes strongly of mango and orange, 3 to 5 days.

3. Strain the mixture with a mesh strainer into a clean quart jar. Do not push on the solids to extract more liquid.

4. Stir in the simple syrup.

5. Seal and store in a cool, dark cabinet. Use within 1 year.

VEGETABLE LIQUEURS

THE VERY NOTION OF FLAVORING LIQUEURS WITH VEGETABLES SEEMS ODD. For one thing, liqueurs are sweet by definition, and vegetables definitely are not. In fact, the concept of sweetness is such anathema to our typical notion of vegetables that we have created a whole other culinary category for sweet vegetables — we call them fruit. Rhubarb, for example, isn't a fruit at all, not even botanically. It's a stem, but we call it fruit because it needs sugar to become palatable. On the other hand, a tomato is clearly a fruit — its flesh houses the seeds for its plant — but do we call it thus? No, never; it's verboten.

Or consider cucumbers and watermelons. Botanically both are fruits. Both are green, contain the seeds of their plant, and have a rind surrounding lots of moist, pulpy flesh. The only reason cucumbers are considered vegetables and watermelons are not is that watermelons are sweet.

Once you catch on that the difference between vegetables and fruit is largely semantic, it becomes easy to start messing around with these versatile ingredients. And this chapter is a good place to get your feet wet and your veggies sweetened.

The process is the same, except that in many vegetable liqueurs you add the sugar syrup along with the vegetable for tincturing. Especially with hard, dry vegetables like carrots, sweet potatoes, and beets, adding the syrup early ensures that there is enough moisture in the tincture to capture all of the flavorful elements.

Hard fruits and vegetables also need a longer tincturing time to break down fibers and release those flavorful components, so you will see that many vegetable liqueurs go through the tincturing process for more than a week.

It is especially fun to play with the savory elements in vegetables — meaty flavors in mushrooms; bitter alkaloids in endive, artichoke, and radicchio: and creamy-starchy components in potatoes and corn. It's enlightening to expose the natural fruity sweetness of bell peppers, tomatoes, and beets. Cucumbers, fennel, and celery lend clean vegetal refreshment to their liqueurs, while arugula reveals more of its spicy personality when reduced to pure flavor.

Sweet-Pepper Surprise

In a class of vegetables where status is measured in Scoville units, the perennially pleasant, unchallenging, heat-free sweet bell pepper wins the Ms. Congeniality award hands down. Red bell peppers are just ripe green peppers, and like all ripe fruit they are juicier, sweeter, and more aromatic than their younger counterparts. But when this nice girl of capsicums is infused into pepper-scented reposado tequila, perfumed with orange oil, and sweetened with cactus syrup, she takes her rightful place as the saucy señorita of potent potables.

MAKES ABOUT 1 QUART

2 cups vodka (80–100 proof)
1 cup reposado tequila (80 proof)
3 red bell peppers, stemmed, seeded, and chopped
Grated zest of 1 orange
1 cup agave syrup

1. Combine the vodka, tequila, bell peppers, orange zest, and agave syrup in a half-gallon jar. Stir to moisten everything.

2. Seal the jar and put it in a cool, dark cabinet until the liquid smells and tastes strongly of bell pepper, about 7 days.

3. Strain the mixture with a mesh strainer into a clean quart jar. Do not push on the solids to extract more liquid.

4. Seal and store in a cool, dark cabinet. Use within 1 year.

Y *L'chaim!* *Use in a supernatural Bloody Mary, a Manhattan Rustico (page 246), or a Capsaicin Cocktail (page 251).*

Gingergold

In vegetable commerce, carotene is gold. The herald of vitamins C and A, a pure gold color ensures nutrition and natural sweetness. In this gilded liqueur, the color and flavor of ripe yellow bell peppers and carrots combine with the aroma from a small amount of fresh ginger to form a sweet and spicy triumvirate.

MAKES ABOUT 1 QUART

2 cups golden rum (80 proof)

1 cup vodka (80–100 proof)

2 yellow bell peppers, stemmed, seeded, and chopped

2 carrots, peeled, ends trimmed, and coarsely shredded

1 (1-inch) piece fresh ginger, finely shredded

1 cup Simple Syrup (page 24)

1. Combine the rum, vodka, bell peppers, carrots, and ginger in a half-gallon jar. Stir to moisten everything.

2. Seal the jar and put it in a cool, dark cabinet until the liquid smells and tastes strongly of bell pepper and ginger, 7 to 10 days.

3. Strain the mixture with a mesh strainer into a clean quart jar. Do not push on the solids to extract more liquid.

4. Stir in the simple syrup.

5. Seal and store in a cool, dark cabinet. Use within 1 year.

Y *Santé!* *Rely on this liqueur's benign power in a Martini or Golden Caipirinha (page 246).*

Rüt

There are root beers, root whiskey, and complex aromatic liqueurs that use licorice root or sassafras in their secret formulas, but I believe this is the first alcoholic dram to be made from 100 percent vegetal root stock. It is earthy and terrestrially sweet, primal, and fertile — the tipple of preindustrial man. Employ its primordial power to reinvigorate an Old-Fashioned or inebriate a classic root beer float.

MAKES ABOUT 1 QUART

1 fifth (750 ml/3¼ cups) rye (80 proof)

2 parsnips, peeled, ends trimmed, and coarsely shredded

2 carrots, peeled, ends trimmed, and coarsely shredded

1 beet, peeled, ends trimmed, and coarsely shredded

2 tablespoons finely shredded fresh horseradish

1 cup Brown Simple Syrup (page 24)

1. Combine the rye, parsnips, carrots, beet, horseradish, and simple syrup in a half-gallon jar. Stir to moisten the vegetables.

2. Seal the jar and put it in a cool, dark cabinet until the liquid smells and tastes strongly of root vegetables, about 7 days.

3. Strain the mixture with a mesh strainer into a clean quart jar. Do not push on the solids to extract more liquid.

4. Seal and store in a cool, dark cabinet. Use within 1 year.

Y *Bottoms Up!* *See Rooted Old-Fashioned (page 249) and Rüt Beer Float (page 255).*

Sugar Beet

Beets are sweet (beet sugar is the second most common sweet-ener on the planet), but you'd never know it by the way my mom cooked them. Dirt tasted better. The trick to capturing the natural candy-like quality of beets is to trap the sugar. If you are eating the vegetable, that means keeping the beet away from liquid, which dissolves the sugar. If you're drinking your beets, it means soaking them in sweetened alcohol until they relinquish their ruby hue and stored sugar into the spirit.

MAKES ABOUT 1 QUART

1 fifth (750 ml/3¼ cups) light rum (80 proof)

4 red beets, peeled, ends trimmed, and coarsely shredded

Grated zest and juice of 1 orange

1 cup Simple Syrup (page 24)

1. Combine the rum, beets, orange zest, and simple syrup in a half-gallon jar. Stir to moisten everything.

2. Seal the jar and put it in a cool, dark cabinet until the liquid smells and tastes strongly of beets, about 7 days.

3. Strain the mixture with a mesh strainer into a clean quart jar. Do not push on the solids to extract more liquid.

4. Seal and store in a cool, dark cabinet. Use within 1 year.

Y *Salut!* *Use liberally to rouge a Cosmopolitan.*

Smoky Bacon Bourbon

Many experiments fail, thereby teaching you what you don't know and pushing you to further experimentation. But sometimes the most far-fetched experiments yield surprisingly down-to-earth results. That is the case with my sojourns into the realm of bacon-potato liqueur. The yellow potatoes lend texture and a gentle golden glow, while the bacon blends elegantly with the bourbon and brown sugar, producing a sweet and savory, slightly smoky bourbon liqueur with a creamy finish.

MAKES ABOUT 1 QUART

1 fifth (750 ml/3¼ cups) bourbon
    (80 proof)
3 golden potatoes, peeled and
    coarsely shredded
6 strips apple-smoked bacon, cooked
    until crisp, blotted dry and crumbled
    Pinch of smoked salt, like
    hickory- or apple-smoked
2 tablespoons celery seeds
1 cup Brown Simple Syrup (page 24)

1. Combine the bourbon, potatoes, bacon, smoked salt, and celery seeds in a half-gallon jar. Stir to moisten everything.

2. Seal the jar and put it in a cool, dark cabinet until the liquid smells and tastes strongly of vegetables and subtly of bacon, 10 to 14 days.

3. Strain the mixture with a mesh strainer lined with dampened cheesecloth into a clean quart jar. Do not push on the solids to extract more liquid.

4. Stir in the simple syrup.

5. Seal and store in a cool, dark cabinet. Use within 1 year.

Y *Prost!* *Drink as you would Wild Turkey or any bourbon-based liquor.*

Garden Mint

Mint is the veritable flavor of fresh. Just try finding a mainstream toothpaste flavored with anything else. One would think that you couldn't get fresher than mint-scented liqueur, but pairing mint with cucumber raises the freshness ante exponentially. In liqueurs, mint can taste candied. Tying it to the bright crispness of cucumber eliminates any candy connection, leaving you as refreshed as a walk in a mentholated garden.

MAKES ABOUT 1 QUART

1½ cups vodka (80–100 proof)
1½ cups dry vermouth (18% ABV)
2 medium English cucumbers, shredded
1 bunch (2 ounces) fresh mint,
    chopped (about ½ cup)
  Grated zest of 1 lemon
1 cup Simple Syrup (page 24)

1. Combine the vodka, vermouth, cucumbers, mint, and lemon zest in a half-gallon jar. Stir to moisten everything.

2. Seal the jar and put it in a cool, dark cabinet until the liquid smells and tastes strongly of mint, 3 to 5 days.

3. Strain the mixture with a mesh strainer into a clean quart jar. Do not push on the solids to extract more liquid.

4. Stir in the simple syrup.

5. Seal and store in a cool, dark cabinet. Use within 1 year.

Y *Skål!* *Invigorate a Bloody Mary, brighten up gin in a Mint and Soda, pictured, (page 255), or mentholate the standard Cucumber Martini (pages 247 and 248).*

Vegetable Liqueurs

Artichoke

Copycat Cynar

Artichokes have the disturbing quality of making anything eaten after them taste artificially sweet, as if the food had been dusted with saccharin. The culprit is cynarin, a phenolic compound that inhibits the sweet receptors in our taste buds. When the chemical is swept off the tongue by a bite of a different food, the receptors reignite and we taste the difference.

The same phenols make raw artichokes taste bitter and astringent, qualities that disappear when they are cooked but that are exacerbated when tincturing raw artichokes in alcohol. Decidedly astringent and bitter, artichoke liqueur is a potent digestif.

MAKES ABOUT 1 QUART

1 fifth (750 ml/3¼ cups) vodka (80-100 proof)

3 medium globe artichokes, finely chopped in a food processor

Grated zest of 2 lemons

1 cup Simple Syrup (page 24)

1. Combine the vodka, artichokes, and lemon zest in a half-gallon jar. Stir to moisten everything.

2. Seal the jar and put it in a cool, dark cabinet until the liquid smells and tastes strongly of artichoke, 7 to 10 days.

3. Strain the mixture with a mesh strainer into a clean quart jar. Do not push on the solids to extract more liquid.

4. Stir in the simple syrup.

5. Seal and store in a cool, dark cabinet. Use within 1 year.

Y *Sláinte!* *Sip straight up or on the rocks after a large meal. Or any meal.*

Radicchio Campari

Vegetables employ bitterness for defense, to discourage animals from eating them. Farmers have tried for centuries to diminish the bitter alkaloids in such vegetables as eggplant, cucumbers, and cabbages, but in some vegetables, bitterness is prized, as is the case with radicchio and other chicories. The liqueurs that contain these alkaloids are renowned for their ability to aid digestion and improve general health.

Campari is a classic Italian digestive liqueur blended from multiple herbs. It has a bright carmine color, traditionally derived from the shells of cochineal insects. No need for bugs in our version, in which rose-hued radicchio produces a beautiful magenta tint. The round Chioggia heads are the most commonly available.

MAKES ABOUT 1 QUART

1 cup vodka (80-100 proof)
2 cups sweet (red) vermouth (18% ABV)
4 heads Chioggia radicchio, coarsely chopped
  Grated zest of 1 lemon
1 cup Simple Syrup (page 24)

1. Combine the vodka, vermouth, radicchio, and lemon zest in a half-gallon jar. Stir to moisten everything.

2. Seal the jar and put it in a cool, dark cabinet until the liquid smells and tastes strongly of radicchio, about 7 days.

3. Strain the mixture with a mesh strainer into a clean quart jar. Do not push on the solids to extract more liquid.

4. Stir in the simple syrup.

5. Seal and store in a cool, dark cabinet. Use within 1 year.

Y *Cheers!* Makes a radical Negroni.

Sweet-Heat Firewater

Sweetness and heat are companions and competitors, vying for your attention in an endless cycle of pain and relief. In most recipes the two are kept separate, but when forced to share, they can be a raucous culinary couple. This liqueur is a case in point. Made from tequila infused with chiles and sweetened with agave, its perfume arises from an earthy influx of toasted cumin and the volatile aromatic oils in the chiles you choose — woody ancho, floral guajillo, meaty habanero, or acidic pequin.

Capturing those aromas in the alcohol goes hand in hand with the ascendency of heat in the liqueur. In taking time for the aromas to build, you run the risk of producing a tincture of incendiary power. I suggest tasting after a day and deciding how much longer your palate can stand.

MAKES ABOUT 1 QUART

1 fifth (750 ml/3¼ cups) blanco tequila (80 proof)

6 whole dried chiles, like ancho, guajillo, habanero, pequin, or any combination, broken into pieces

3 tablespoons toasted cumin seeds

1 cup agave syrup

1. Combine the tequila, chiles, and cumin seeds in a half-gallon jar. Stir to moisten everything.

2. Seal the jar and put it in a cool, dark cabinet until the liquid smells and tastes strongly of chiles, 1 to 2 days.

3. Strain the mixture with a mesh strainer into a clean quart jar. Do not push on the solids to extract more liquid.

4. Stir in the agave syrup.

5. Seal and store in a cool, dark cabinet. Use within 1 year.

Y *L'chaim!* Makes an awesome Bloody Maria (page 241) and a three-alarm Flaming Lemonade (page 244).

Corny Corn "Liquor"

Fresh corn is as sweet as any apple or berry, and yet we barely think of it as a sweet ingredient. Since the 1960s, the fresh corn market has been dominated by super-sweet varieties that are about 40 percent sugar and only 5 percent starch, making them perfect for liqueurs, especially when using a corn-based liquor like bourbon for your base. This delightful spirit has a silky mouthfeel and a natural sweetness that makes it decidedly easy to drink.

MAKES ABOUT 1 QUART

4 cups corn kernels, fresh (about 4 ears) or frozen, pureed

½ cup Simple Syrup (page 24)

Big pinch of crushed red pepper flakes

1 fifth (750 ml/3¼ cups) bourbon (80 proof)

½ cup honey

1. Combine the corn kernels and simple syrup in a medium saucepan. Heat to boiling over medium heat, stirring often. Let cool completely.

2. Combine the corn mixture, pepper flakes, bourbon, and honey in a half-gallon jar. Stir briefly.

3. Seal the jar and put it in a cool, dark cabinet until the liquid smells and tastes strongly of corn, 3 to 5 days.

4. Strain the mixture with a mesh strainer into a clean quart jar. Do not push on the solids to extract more liquid.

5. Seal and store in a cool, dark cabinet. Use within 1 year.

Y *Santé!* *Use it in a Bourbon Milk Punch (page 239) or a Kiss on the Lips (1 part bourbon and 3 parts apricot nectar).*

Red Lightning

If you could rarify gazpacho, ridding it of its crunchy chunks and infusing its essence into a potable spirit, you would have Red Lightning. Spicy and garden fresh, this is a truly delicious concoction. Drink it over ice as shown, or use it as a base for a Bloody Mary or a vegetable Margarita.

MAKES ABOUT 1 QUART

1½   cups vodka (80–100 proof)
1½   cups reposado tequila (80 proof)
3   large tomatoes, chopped
2   cucumbers, peeled and coarsely shredded
1   red bell pepper, stemmed, seeded, and chopped
1   fresh red chile, stemmed, seeded, and minced
1   tablespoon celery seeds
    Finely grated zest of 1 lemon
½   cup Simple Syrup (page 24)

1. Combine the vodka, tequila, tomatoes, cucumbers, bell pepper, chile, celery seeds, and lemon zest in a half-gallon jar. Stir to moisten everything.

2. Seal the jar and put it in a cool, dark cabinet until the liquid smells and tastes strongly of vegetables, about 7 days.

3. Strain the mixture with a mesh strainer into a clean quart jar. Do not push on the solids to extract more liquid.

4. Stir in the simple syrup.

5. Seal and store in a cool, dark cabinet. Use within 1 year.

Y *Salut!* Mix up a Red Skies at Night (page 242).

Tomato Essence

Intensely flavored yet barely there, tomato water, an extract of tomatoes and salt, became the darling of four-star chefs across the country in the mid-1990s. Like most food fads, it appeared everywhere for a while and then it vanished. Today it resurfaces occasionally, mostly as a tool of mixologists, which is right where we want it.

The process of making tomato water (chopping up a pile of tomatoes, salting them, wrapping them in cheesecloth, and waiting for gravity to extract their essence) is made far more efficient by replacing gravity with alcohol. When it comes to flavor, the attracting power of alcohol far exceeds Newton's favorite force. The resulting liqueur is almost clear but intensely tomatoey.

MAKES ABOUT 1 QUART

1 fifth (750 ml/3¼ cups) vodka
   (80–100 proof)
6 tomatoes, chopped
1 tablespoon celery seeds
   Grated zest of 1 lemon
   Big pinch of sea salt
½ cup Simple Syrup (page 24)

1. Combine the vodka, tomatoes, celery seeds, lemon zest, and salt in a half-gallon jar. Stir to moisten everything.

2. Seal the jar and put it in a cool, dark cabinet until the liquid smells and tastes strongly of tomato, 5 to 7 days.

3. Strain the mixture with a mesh strainer into a clean quart jar. Do not push on the solids to extract more liquid.

4. Stir in the simple syrup.

5. Seal and store in a cool, dark cabinet. Use within 1 year.

Y *Prost!* *Serve chilled in a rarified Bloody Mary or mix up a Niçoise (page 252).*

Rocket Launch

Arugula (known as salad rocket outside North America) has grown in the poor soil of the Mediterranean since Roman times. It serves as the pungent and spicy base for a peppery digestif called Rucolino made on the island of Ischia in the Gulf of Naples. It was touted as a powerful aphrodisiac herb by Virgil and throughout the medieval period, but is now most commonly used as an innocent salad green. I think in truth that its power lies somewhere in between.

MAKES ABOUT 1 QUART

1   fifth (750 ml/3¼ cups) English-
    style gin (80 proof)
4   cups arugula
    Grated zest and juice of 1 lime
    Pinch of sea salt
1   cup Simple Syrup (page 24)

1. Combine the gin, arugula, lime zest and juice, and salt in a half-gallon jar. Stir to moisten everything.

2. Seal the jar and put it in a cool, dark cabinet until the liquid smells and tastes strongly of arugula, 5 to 7 days.

3. Strain the mixture with a mesh strainer into a clean quart jar. Do not push on the solids to extract more liquid.

4. Stir in the simple syrup.

5. Seal and store in a cool, dark cabinet. Use within 1 year.

Y *Skål! Serve over ice before or after a meal in the same way you would serve any herbal digestif.*

Vegetable Liqueurs

Finocchio

Licorice-like flavors are ubiquitous in the manufacturing of liqueurs. There are probably more anise/fennel/licorice-flavored liqueurs than any other single flavor base. Within that family of inebriating elixirs, which includes such regal names as anisette, Pernod, ouzo, and absinthe, this style of fennel liqueur, made principally from fennel bulbs, is the lightest and freshest.

MAKES ABOUT 1 QUART

1 fifth (750 ml/3¼ cups)
  vodka (80-100 proof)
1 fennel bulb, coarsely chopped
3 tablespoons fennel seeds, crushed
¾ cup Simple Syrup (page 24)

1. Combine the vodka, fennel bulb, and fennel seeds in a half-gallon jar. Stir to moisten everything.

2. Seal the jar and put it in a cool, dark cabinet until the liquid smells and tastes strongly of fennel, about 7 days.

3. Strain the mixture with a mesh strainer into a clean quart jar. Do not push on the solids to extract more liquid.

4. Stir in the simple syrup.

5. Seal and store in a cool, dark cabinet. Use within 1 year.

Y *Sláinte!* *Use for a switcheroo on a Screwdriver or Italian Kamikaze (page 252).*

Yammy

Scooping out and gorging on the rich, creamy flesh of baked sweet potatoes is so intrinsic to our notion of its pleasures that it overshadows our perception of its flavor, which we think of as equally rich and creamy. In actuality it is sweet, clean, and nutty. In this liqueur, the corporeal flesh turns to spirit, and that fresh rooty flavor comes through. It is supported with traditional yam-flavoring agents: ginger, orange, honey, and brown sugar.

MAKES ABOUT 1 QUART

1½ cups bourbon (80 proof)

1½ cups dark rum (80 proof)

3 sweet potatoes, peeled and coarsely shredded

1 (3-inch) piece fresh ginger, coarsely shredded

Grated zest of 2 oranges

2 cinnamon sticks, cracked

½ cup honey

½ cup Brown Simple Syrup (page 24)

1. Combine the bourbon, rum, sweet potatoes, ginger, orange zest, cinnamon, honey, and simple syrup in a half-gallon jar. Stir to moisten everything.

2. Seal the jar and put it in a cool, dark cabinet until the liquid has a creamy mouthfeel and smells and tastes strongly of ginger, cinnamon, and orange , about 7 days.

3. Strain the mixture with a mesh strainer into a clean quart jar. Do not push on the solids to extract more liquid.

4. Seal and store in a cool, dark cabinet. Use within 1 year.

Y **Prost!** *Use as base for an Old-Fashioned or Manhattan.*

Cool as a Cuke

In the world of beverages, refreshment abounds, but not so much in the land of liqueurs. Liqueurs are generally spoken of in terms of flavor impact, mouthfeel, and potency. This liqueur changes that. Like its namesake, it is cool and clean and crisp, a liquid cucumber essence. I'm sure there are tons of cocktails that would benefit from it, but I can't stop drinking Cucumber Martinis long enough to think of any.

MAKES ABOUT 1 QUART

1 fifth (750 ml/3¼ cups) Dutch-style gin (80 proof)

4 medium English cucumbers, ends trimmed and coarsely shredded

8 fresh dill sprigs

Pinch of sea salt

¾ cup Simple Syrup (page 24)

1. Combine the gin, cucumbers, dill, and salt in a half-gallon jar. Stir to moisten everything.

2. Seal the jar and put it in a cool, dark cabinet until the liquid smells and tastes strongly of cucumber, about 7 days.

3. Strain the mixture with a mesh strainer into a clean quart jar. Do not push on the solids to extract more liquid.

4. Stir in the simple syrup.

5. Seal and store in a cool, dark cabinet. Use within 1 year.

Y *L'chaim!* *See Cucumber Martini 2 (page 248). And I did think of one more — the Archangel (page 247).*

CelRay Surprise

Celery is another definitively refreshing vegetable, but unlike cucumber it has a long beverage tradition. Dr. Brown's Cel-Ray tonic was first manufactured in 1868 in Brooklyn, New York, as a therapeutic beverage. There is no evidence that it had medicinal powers or that there ever was a Dr. Brown, but the flavor stuck. It is still being produced today, and this is my inebriated tribute. Unlike the soda, which is strongly flavored with celery seed, this liqueur is fresher, deriving its flavor largely from cucumber, celery, and green tomato.

MAKES ABOUT 1 QUART

1 fifth (750 ml/3¼ cups) Dutch-style gin (80 proof)

8 celery stalks, finely chopped

2 medium English cucumbers, ends trimmed and coarsely shredded

1 green (or very underripe) tomato, chopped

1 tablespoon celery seeds

Big pinch of sea salt

¾ cup Simple Syrup (page 24)

1. Combine the gin, celery, cucumbers, tomato, celery seeds, and salt in a half-gallon jar. Stir to moisten everything.

2. Seal the jar and put it in a cool, dark cabinet until the liquid smells and tastes strongly of celery and cucumber, about 7 days.

3. Strain the mixture with a mesh strainer into a clean quart jar. Do not push on the solids to extract more liquid.

4. Stir in the simple syrup.

5. Seal and store in a cool, dark cabinet. Use within 1 year.

⋯⋯⋯⋯⋯⋯⋯⋯⋯⋯⋯⋯⋯⋯⋯⋯⋯⋯⋯⋯⋯⋯⋯⋯⋯⋯⋯⋯

🍸 *Bottoms Up!* *Drink in the summer with a long spritz of seltzer over plenty of ice in a tall glass, or try a CelRay Tonic (page 255).*

Pumpkin Pie

Raw ingredients are usually preferable for flavoring liqueurs, as uncooked flavors are less adulterated and generally stronger, but the flavor of pumpkin pie has little to do with raw pumpkin, so it is necessary to start with a cooked product when concocting this liqueur. I could ask you to cook up some pumpkin, but canned pumpkin is already cooked. All you need to do is add pie-style sweeteners and seasonings, and the essence of autumnal feasting is in the glass.

MAKES ABOUT 1 QUART

1½ cups bourbon (80 proof)

1½ cups vodka (80 proof)

1 (15-ounce) can pumpkin purée (not pumpkin pie filling)

1 (1-inch) piece fresh ginger, coarsely shredded

½ vanilla bean (Madagascar or Bourbon), split

2 cinnamon sticks, cracked

1 cup Caramelized Simple Syrup (page 24)

1. Combine the bourbon, vodka, pumpkin, ginger, vanilla, cinnamon, and simple syrup in a half-gallon jar. Stir to moisten everything.

2. Seal the jar and put it in a cool, dark cabinet until the liquid smells and tastes strongly of pumpkin and spices, about 7 days.

3. Strain the mixture with a mesh strainer lined with damp cheesecloth into a clean quart jar. Do not push on the solids to extract more liquid.

4. Seal and store in a cool, dark cabinet. Use within 1 year.

⅂ *Sláinte!* *Use this spiced liqueur as a base for eggnog, serve it gently warmed like mulled wine, or mix up a glass of Pumpkin Spice (page 251).*

Primeval

There is nothing tame about this liqueur. Coarse, rustic rye whiskey is infused with dried morels and porcini mushrooms, a handful of bruised juniper berries, and a two-finger pinch of dried thyme. The aroma is of fallen logs half submerged in moss and lichen, unfolding ferns, and mushrooms sprouting in the dark. Sipping it is like tres-passing in a primeval forest — unexplored and very far from home.

MAKES A LITTLE MORE THAN 1 PINT

1 fifth (750 ml/3¼ cups) rye (80 proof)

24 juniper berries, crushed

¼ cup dried morel mushrooms, broken into small pieces

¼ cup dried porcini mushrooms, broken into small pieces

1 teaspoon dried thyme

Big pinch of sea salt

¾ cup Brown Simple Syrup (page 24)

1. Combine the rye, juniper berries, morel and porcini mushrooms, thyme, salt, and simple syrup in a half-gallon jar. Stir to moisten everything.

2. Seal the jar and put it in a cool, dark cabinet until the liquid smells and tastes strongly, about 7 days.

3. Strain the mixture with a mesh strainer into a clean quart jar. Do not push on the solids to extract more liquid.

4. Seal and store in a cool, dark cabinet. Use within 1 year.

Y **Cheers!** *Perfect for a paleolithic Old-Fashioned.*

Sunny Splash

Jerusalem artichokes (a.k.a. sunchokes), the vegetable base for this sweet and spicy liqueur, are neither artichokes nor native to Jerusalem. Originally from North America, they were cultivated by Native Americans long before the arrival of Europeans. They got their artichoke moniker when the French explorer Samuel de Champlain sent them back to France in 1605, where their taste was compared to that of an artichoke bottom.

The comparison is not inaccurate. In this liqueur, the sunchokes are amended with shredded carrot for color and complementary flavor, and some ginger for a little kick.

MAKES ABOUT 1 QUART

1 fifth (750 ml/3¼ cups) vodka
   (80-100 proof)

8 ounces sunchokes (Jerusalem
   artichokes), coarsely shredded

2 carrots, peeled, ends trimmed,
   and coarsely shredded

1 (1-inch) piece fresh ginger,
   coarsely shredded

¾ cup Simple Syrup (page 24)

1. Combine the vodka, sunchokes, carrots, ginger, and simple syrup in a half-gallon jar. Stir to moisten everything.

2. Seal the jar and put it in a cool, dark cabinet until the liquid has a strong vegetal gingery aroma, about 7 days.

3. Strain the mixture with a mesh strainer into a clean quart jar. Do not push on the solids to extract more liquid.

4. Seal and store in a cool, dark cabinet. Use within 1 year.

Y *Bottoms Up!* *An ingenious spike for lemonade and a natural mixed with orange juice and a splash of ginger ale, it also makes a Liquid Sunshine (page 251).*

Sweet Pea

Wee sweet spring peas make ethereally refreshing liqueurs — the closest sensation to imbibing the fertile promise of spring. But unless you are committed to planting peas as soon as the threat of frost is gone, you will be hard pressed to find a fresh sweet pea any time before July. Your alternative is to use sugar snap peas (an edible pod pea, similar to snow peas) or rely on frozen peas, which tend to be much younger and sweeter than the fresh peas that are available in most produce markets.

This emerald green liqueur exploits the classic pairing of peas and mint. Sip it on a hot summer night when the setting sun invites you to step outdoors.

MAKES ABOUT 1 QUART

2½ cups vodka (80-100 proof)
1 cup dry vermouth (18% ABV)
1 pound sugar snap peas or frozen green peas, finely chopped
1 bunch (2 ounces) fresh mint, chopped (about ½ cup)
Finely grated zest of 1 lemon
Pinch (⅛ teaspoon) fine sea salt
1¼ cups Simple Syrup (page 24)
2 drops green food coloring
1 drop yellow food coloring

1. Combine the vodka, vermouth, peas, mint, lemon zest, salt, and simple syrup in a half-gallon jar. Stir to moisten everything.

2. Seal the jar and put it in a cool, dark cabinet until the liquid smells and tastes like a blend of peas and mint, 3 to 4 days.

3. Strain the mixture with a mesh strainer into a clean jar. Do not push on the solids to extract more liquid.

4. Allow the strained liquid to sit overnight; sediment will sink to the bottom.

5. Decant or rack the clear liquid from the sediment into a clean quart jar.

6. Stir in the food coloring, seal the jar and store in a cool, dark cabinet. Use within 1 year.

HERB & SPICE LIQUEURS

Herb liqueurs were the original medicinal tonics. All plants are adept at biochemical invention, and capturing those chemicals in alcohol is the basis of pharmacology.

Herbs and spices contain potent compounds called phenolics and terpenes that work in two ways: 1) preventing cellular damage, particularly to cell DNA, and 2) acting as anti-inflammatory agents by moderating the body's reactions to cell damage, which otherwise might contribute to the development of cancer and heart disease. The phenolic compounds in oregano, dill, bay leaf, rosemary, and turmeric, for example, are well known for their anti-inflammatory properties.

We can obtain these compounds by eating lots of spices and herbs, but the amount we would have to consume to ensure health is daunting. It's far better to concentrate those medicinal (and flavorful and colorful) properties in a tincture of alcohol, where the benefits of these potent botanical pharmaceuticals become readily available.

ABSINTHE MAKES THE HEART...

Though the transition of liqueurs from medicine to libation was gradual, it exploded in late nineteenth-century France with the popular introduction of "the green fairy" (*la fée verte*) or absinthe, a vibrantly green, high-proof, licorice-flavored spirit. Its popularity brought about scores of imitators, which is the reason that a disproportionate number of liqueurs have a licorice flavor base.

Manet, Toulouse-Lautrec, Baudelaire, Rimbaud, and Oscar Wilde were all huge fans of the stuff, and touted it as a wellspring of lucidity and creativity, giving absinthe a connection with bohemian artists and art that continues today.

Absinthe is flavored with anise and fennel seeds and tinted with a profusion of herbs and flowers, one of which, wormwood (*Artemesia absinthium*), made the popular liqueur infamous. In 1905, a Swiss laborer named Jean LaFray went on a bender after work, downing a considerable amount of wine and spirits, including several glasses of absinthe. Upon returning home he murdered his wife and children, and in media reports, absinthe was blamed for turning LaFray mad and precipitating the murders. Within a few years, absinthe had been banned in Switzerland, many other European countries, and the United States.

The ban, now lifted in many places, centered on thujone, a chemical component of wormwood. High concentrations of thujone were thought to cause hallucinations among absinthe drinkers. Current studies show that thujone causes neurons to fire more easily, improving cognitive functions like thinking and memory. In extremely high doses, thujone can cause muscle spasms and convulsions. However, the strongest absinthes contain less than 4.3 mg per liter.

The psychoactive effects of absinthe are more likely attributable to its high alcohol content (about 68 percent, or 140 proof). In the United States, foods or beverages made with wormwood must be free of thujone, even though several other herbs, notably sage, contain the chemical.

Anisette

In the wake of absinthe frenzy (see Absinthe Makes the Heart . . . , facing page), hundreds of anise-flavored liqueurs were produced in France; anisette is an umbrella term for all of them. This version combines two forms of anise: anise seed (also spelled aniseed), which is the small seed of a flowering plant that grows in temperate climates throughout the world, and star anise, the dried fruit of an evergreen tree native to Vietnam and China. The spices are botanically unrelated but share a common chemical compound, anethole, which gives them a similar flavor. Anethole is also present in fennel.

MAKES ABOUT 1 QUART

1 fifth (750 ml/3¼ cups) vodka (80–100 proof)

1 cup anise seeds, crushed

12 star anise, cracked

1 cup Simple Syrup (page 24)

1. Combine the vodka, anise seeds, and star anise seed in a half-gallon jar. Stir to moisten everything.

2. Seal the jar and put it in a cool, dark cabinet until the liquid smells and tastes strongly of anise, 1 to 3 days.

3. Strain the mixture with a mesh strainer into a clean quart jar. Do not push on the solids to extract more liquid.

4. Stir in the simple syrup.

5. Seal and store in a cool, dark cabinet. Use within 1 year.

Y *L'chaim!* Mix up make an Apertivo (page 245) or an Italian Kamikaze (page 252).

Herb-Santé

Copycat Herbsaint

Yet another anise-flavored absinthe knock-off, Herbsaint is made by the Sazerac Company in New Orleans. Originally produced by J.M. Legendre & Co, it was called Legendre Absinthe, but the name was changed when the Federal Alcohol Control Administration objected to the sale of "absinthe." Herbsaint never contained wormwood, so there was no violation of law, but the name was changed to Legendre Herbsaint. This version, cleverly renamed to avoid trademark violation, is also wormwood-free.

MAKES ABOUT 1 QUART

1 cup vodka (80-100 proof)

2 cups dry vermouth (18% ABV)

1 cup chopped fresh flat-leaf parsley

½ cup anise seeds, crushed

½ cup chopped fresh basil

¼ cup chopped fresh tarragon

¼ cup chopped fresh rosemary leaves

1 cup Simple Syrup (page 24)

1. Combine the vodka, vermouth, parsley, anise seeds, basil, tarragon, and rosemary in a half-gallon jar. Stir to moisten everything.

2. Seal the jar and put it in a cool, dark cabinet until the liquid smells and tastes strongly of herbs, 3 to 5 days.

3. Strain the mixture with a mesh strainer into a clean quart jar. Do not push on the solids to extract more liquid.

4. Stir in the simple syrup.

5. Seal and store in a cool, dark cabinet. Use within 1 year.

. . . .

Y **Bottoms Up!** *This is a classic choice for making a Brandy Sazerac, pictured (page 249), or an Allied Forces (page 247), or La Verenne (page 255).*

Provençal

The arid central hills of Provence are far from fertile, yet they are awash in herbs, including lavender, thyme, sage, and savory, and the bees that feed off the wildflower nectar produce a vast amount of honey. This fragrant liqueur is pale green, light, and airy — an interplay of honey, lavender, orange, rosemary, and fennel. As in most herbal liqueurs, the balance is delicate. It is pleasant sipped simply from stemware late in the afternoon, and it makes an effective replacement for vermouth in Martinis and Manhattans.

MAKES ABOUT 1 QUART

1   fifth (750 ml/3¼ cups) vodka
     (80-100 proof)
¼   cup fennel seeds, crushed
3   tablespoons dried lavender blossoms
3   tablespoons fresh rosemary
     leaves, crushed
     Finely grated zest of 1 orange
½   cup mild honey, such as wildflower
     or orange blossom
½   cup Simple Syrup (page 24)

1. Combine the vodka, fennel seeds, lavender, rosemary, orange zest, and honey in a half-gallon jar. Stir to moisten everything.

2. Seal the jar. Put it in a cool, dark cabinet until the liquid smells and tastes strongly of orange and rosemary, 3 to 5 days.

3. Strain the mixture with a mesh strainer into a clean quart jar. Do not push on the solids to extract more liquid.

4. Stir in the simple syrup.

5. Seal and store in a cool, dark cabinet. Use within 1 year.

Y **Santé!** *Use to make a Niçoise (page 252).*

Tonic Gin

Gin and Tonic is my go-to summertime inebriant, so it is only natural that I would come up with a way of streamlining my route to bliss by creating tonic-flavored gin. Quinine, the flavoring ingredient in carbonated tonic, comes from cinchona bark. Cinchona is a small tree native to South America that was cultivated by the Quechua people of Peru for medicinal purposes. In the seventeenth century, Jesuit priests began using cinchona to successfully treat the symptoms of malaria. I figure I down enough each summer to have obtained full immunity.

Cinchona is available online in both bark and powder form (see Resources, page 257). The bark is preferable for tincturing.

MAKES ABOUT 1 QUART

1 fifth (750 ml/3¼ cups) gin (80 proof)
½ cup cinchona bark pieces
3 tablespoons juniper berries, crushed
Finely grated zest of 2 limes
1 cup Simple Syrup (page 24)

1. Combine the gin, cinchona bark, juniper berries, and lime zest in a half-gallon jar. Stir to moisten everything.

2. Seal the jar and put it in a cool, dark cabinet until the liquid smells of juniper and lime and tastes strongly bitter, 5 to 7 days.

3. Strain the mixture with a mesh strainer into a clean quart jar. Do not push on the solids to extract more liquid.

4. Stir in the simple syrup.

5. Seal and store in a cool, dark cabinet. Use within 1 year.

Y *Salut!* To make a streamlined Gin and Tonic, pour this liqueur over ice in a tall glass and add seltzer to taste; garnish with lime.

Sorta Strega

Copycat Strega

Strega, a digestif strongly flavored with mint and fennel, has been made in Benevento, Italy, since 1860. Similar to Galliano but less yellow, it is syrupy-sweet and has a lingering coniferous finish. Its pale yellow-green color comes from saffron. Strega is Italian for "witch," connecting the liqueur to the legends of witchcraft that have been flying around Benevento for centuries.

MAKES ABOUT 1 QUART

1 cup vodka (80-100 proof)

3 cups dry vermouth (18% ABV)

1 cup chopped fresh mint

½ cup chopped fresh rosemary leaves

¼ cup chopped fresh basil

¼ cup fennel seeds, crushed

¼ cup chopped fresh tarragon

Grated zest of 2 lemons

Pinch of saffron threads

1 cup Simple Syrup (page 24)

1. Combine the vodka, vermouth, mint, rosemary, basil, fennel seeds, tarragon, lemon zest, and saffron in a half-gallon jar. Stir to moisten everything.

2. Seal the jar and put it in a cool, dark cabinet until the liquid smells and tastes strongly of herbs, 3 to 5 days.

3. Strain the mixture with a mesh strainer into a clean quart jar. Do not push on the solids to extract more liquid.

4. Stir in the simple syrup.

5. Seal and store in a cool, dark cabinet. Use within 1 year.

Y *Prost!* *Classically sipped from thimble-sized stemware as a digestif.*

Orange Rosemary

If coming of age in 2009 counts as classic, then this inspired combination of orange and rosemary is pure classicism. Rosemary is strong, and when paired with other herbs it inevitably dominates, but team it with orange and the two spar and embrace as worthy collaborators. Fortunately for us, both flavors are volatile, tincturing the alcohol quickly.

MAKES ABOUT 1 QUART

1 fifth (750 ml/3¼ cups) vodka
   (80–100 proof)
   Finely grated zest of 6 oranges
¼ cup fresh rosemary leaves, crushed
½ cup honey
½ cup Simple Syrup (page 24)

1. Combine the vodka, orange zest, rosemary, and honey in a half-gallon jar. Stir to moisten everything.

2. Seal the jar and put it in a cool, dark cabinet until the liquid smells and tastes strongly of orange and rosemary, 3 to 5 days.

3. Strain the mixture with a mesh strainer into a clean quart jar. Do not push on the solids to extract more liquid.

4. Stir in the simple syrup.

5. Seal and store in a cool, dark cabinet. Use within 1 year.

Y *Skål!* *Sip as an aperitif accompanied by a salty hors d'oeuvre.*

Cherry Basil

Similar to the orange and rosemary in the previous recipe, sour cherries and basil meet each other as equals. These are intense flavors, and because the combo is unexpected you may imagine the two would resist one another, but soon after the first sip you will not be able to remember a time when basil and cherries was not your favorite flavor combo. I first had it 20 years ago in Chablis as a fruit preserve, and since then it has come to be a favorite in pies and ice cream, and now in this cherry red herbal elixir.

MAKES ABOUT 1 QUART

1 fifth (750 ml/3¼ cups) vodka (80–100 proof)
2 pints sour cherries, stemmed and crushed (no need to remove pits)
1 bunch fresh basil, bruised
1¼ cups Simple Syrup (page 24)

1. Combine the vodka, cherries, and basil in a half-gallon jar. Stir to moisten everything.

2. Seal the jar and put it in a cool, dark cabinet until the liquid smells and tastes strongly of cherries and basil, 3 to 5 days.

3. Strain the mixture with a mesh strainer into a clean quart jar. Do not push on the solids to extract more liquid.

4. Stir in the simple syrup.

5. Seal and store in a cool, dark cabinet. Use within 1 year.

Y *Sláinte!* *For a Black Forest Cosmo, shake 1 part chocolate liqueur and 4 parts Cherry Basil with ice and strain.*

Ginger-Cardamom Mead

Spices usually play supporting roles, enhancing the main attraction rather than taking center stage, but ginger and cardamom are hardly shy. In fact, they can be overpowering on their own, and together you might think they would be positively overwhelming. It turns out that when you give them both the spotlight, they settle down and work together. The results are pretty exciting, with pungent notes of eucalyptus and menthol, a ginger zing, and a whiff of citrus, all slathered in a floral balm of honey. This is strong stuff, but delicious amending a brandy or mixed with bourbon and a spritz of lemon.

MAKES ABOUT 1 QUART

1 fifth (750 ml/3¼ cups) vodka (80–100 proof)
1 cup finely grated fresh ginger
¼ cup green cardamom pods, crushed
2 tablespoons dried thyme
1 cup honey

1. Combine the vodka, ginger, cardamom, thyme, and honey in a half-gallon jar. Stir to moisten everything.

2. Seal the jar and put it in a cool, dark cabinet until the liquid smells and tastes strongly of ginger and cardamom, 3 to 5 days.

3. Strain the mixture with a mesh strainer into a clean quart jar. Do not push on the solids to extract more liquid.

4. Seal and store in a cool, dark cabinet. Use within 1 year.

Y *Santé!* *Try a Twisted Horse's Neck (page 256).*

Angelica

Copycat Chartreuse

There are scores of Angelica species, but only one is commonly used as a flavoring and medicine — the garden angelica (A. archangelica). It is a common flavoring agent of gin and the principal herb in Chartreuse, made by French monks in the Grand Chartreuse monastery. The original formula for Chartreuse supposedly contains 132 herbs, flowers, and spices. Alas, my pale imitation has but 8; only 124 to go. The characteristic green color of Chartreuse comes from the chlorophyll in the bounty of herbs that go into the secret blend.

MAKES ABOUT 1 QUART

1 fifth (750 ml/3¼ cups) vodka (80–100 proof)

½ cup chopped dried angelica root (see Resources)

½ cup blanched almonds, finely chopped

6 allspice berries, cracked

2 cinnamon sticks, cracked

½ of a whole nutmeg, grated

6 star anise, cracked

¼ cup coriander seeds, cracked

3 tablespoons dried marjoram

1 6-ounce bag baby spinach leaves, finely chopped in a food processor

1 cup Simple Syrup (page 24)

3 drops yellow food coloring (optional)

2 drops green food coloring (optional)

1. Combine the vodka, angelica root, almonds, allspice berries, cinnamon, nutmeg, star anise, coriander seeds, marjoram, and spinach in a half-gallon jar. Stir to moisten everything.

2. Seal the jar and put it in a cool, dark cabinet until the liquid smells and tastes strongly of spices, 2 to 3 weeks.

3. Strain the mixture with a mesh strainer into a clean quart jar. Do not push on the solids to extract more liquid.

4. Stir in the simple syrup, and add the food coloring, if using.

5. Seal and store in a cool, dark cabinet. Use within 1 year.

Y **Cheers!** *Drizzle over grilled fish or chicken or use in an herbal marinade.*

Lots of Licorice

Copycat Ouzo

Ouzo, or something like it, has been produced in Greece since the fourteenth century, but it wasn't until the early twentieth century that the ban on absinthe (see page 106) gave this anise-flavored folk liqueur, billed as "absinthe without the wormwood," a chance at international notoriety. Before the 1930s, when most ouzo became 100 percent distilled, the anise flavor could be either tinctured or distilled. Tinctured ouzo has a more rounded, fuller-bodied flavor than distilled products.

MAKES A SKIMPY FIFTH

1 fifth (750 ml/3¼ cups) vodka (80–100 proof)
½ cup licorice root, crushed
¼ cup anise seeds, crushed
12 star anise, cracked
1 cup Simple Syrup (page 24)

1. Combine the vodka, licorice, anise seeds, and star anise in a half-gallon jar. Stir to moisten everything.

2. Seal the jar and put it in a cool, dark cabinet until the liquid smells and tastes strongly of licorice, 3 to 5 days.

3. Strain the mixture with a mesh strainer into a clean quart jar. Do not push on the solids to extract more liquid.

4. Stir in the simple syrup.

5. Seal and store in a cool, dark cabinet. Use within 1 year.

Y *Salut!* Mix with a splash of water for drinking, which turns it from clear to cloudy.

Green Coriander

Most aromatic plants yield either spices (the hard parts — bark, seeds, roots) or herbs (the soft parts — leaves and flowers), but coriander gives us both. The seed is sold as coriander; the leaf is cilantro. This liqueur employs both: the seed for pungency and the leaf for freshness and aroma. Plus there's a good amount of lime oil (from lime zest) for body. Drink it up or splash some over grilled salmon or a pan-seared chicken breast.

MAKES ABOUT 1 QUART

1 fifth (750 ml/3¼ cups) tequila (80 proof)

½ cup coriander seeds, toasted and coarsely ground

1 bunch fresh cilantro, chopped

Finely grated zest of 3 limes

Big pinch of sea salt

1 cup Simple Syrup (page 24)

1. Combine the tequila, coriander seeds, cilantro, lime zest, and salt in a half-gallon jar. Stir to moisten everything.

2. Seal the jar and put it in a cool, dark cabinet until the liquid smells and tastes strongly of coriander, 3 to 5 days.

3. Strain the mixture with a mesh strainer into a clean quart jar. Do not push on the solids to extract more liquid.

4. Stir in the simple syrup.

5. Seal and store in a cool, dark cabinet. Use within 1 year.

Y *Skål!* *Use it to mix up a streamlined Tequila and Tonic; lime already included.*

Herb & Spice Liqueurs

Caraway

Copycat Kümmel

Kümmel *means both "caraway" and "cumin seed" in three languages — German, Dutch, and Yiddish — as well as the liqueur made from them. In the Jewish neighborhood where I was raised, kümmel or kimmel were the seeds that flavored rye bread. But now I've switched over and I'm a liqueur man all the way.*

The seeds that go into this liqueur are highly aromatic, and when cracked they release their flavors quickly. A few hours are all it takes to make a potently fragrant liqueur. In fact, you will need to take care not to tincture for too long or an overpowering mentholated component will develop from the chemical structure of caraway.

MAKES A LITTLE MORE THAN 1 PINT

- 1 fifth (750 ml/3¼ cups) vodka (80-100 proof)
- ½ cup caraway seeds, coarsely cracked
- ½ cup cumin seeds, coarsely cracked
- ½ cup fennel seeds, coarsely cracked
- ¼ cup Simple Syrup (page 24)

1. Combine the vodka, caraway seeds, cumin seeds, and fennel seeds in a half-gallon jar. Stir to moisten everything.

2. Seal the jar and put it in a cool, dark cabinet until the liquid smells and tastes strongly of caraway, cumin and fennel, 4 to 8 hours.

3. Strain the mixture with a mesh strainer into a clean quart jar. Do not push on the solids to extract more liquid.

4. Stir in the simple syrup.

5. Seal and store in a cool, dark cabinet. Use within 1 year.

🍸 ***Bottoms Up!*** *Kümmel is used as a secondary liquor in many cocktails, including the Allied Forces (page 247), a decidedly un-dry gin Martini.*

Aphrodite

We know that alcohol is excellent at picking up flavor molecules and antioxidants from herbs and spices and transporting them into our bodies, but what about latching onto reputed aphrodisiacs? Ginseng root contains ginsenosides, compounds that have been shown to stimulate erectile function in laboratory animals, and pomegranate is supposed to boost fertility. I've been drinking this liqueur for some time, and while I prefer to remain mum on its effects, I can attest that it is beautifully balanced, fruity, and aromatic, and it's a spectacular color — sunset flame.

MAKES ABOUT 1 QUART

- 1 fifth (750 ml/3¼ cups) gin (80 proof)
  Finely grated zest of 3 oranges
  Seeds from 1 pomegranate, bruised
- 4 3-inch pieces of ginseng root, broken into small pieces
- ¼ cup anise seeds, crushed
  Big pinch of sea salt
- 1 cup honey

1. Combine the gin, orange zest, pomegranate seeds, ginseng, anise seeds, and salt in a half-gallon jar. Stir to moisten everything.

2. Seal the jar and put it in a cool, dark cabinet until the liquid smells and tastes strongly of citrus and anise, 3 to 5 days.

3. Strain the mixture with a mesh strainer into a clean quart jar. Do not push on the solids to extract more liquid.

4. Stir in the honey.

5. Seal and store in a cool, dark cabinet. Use within 1 year.

....

Y *Prost!* *Sip it straight anytime or over a rock on a sultry afternoon, or make a Brandy Sazerac (page 249).*

Spicy Rum

Copycat Spiced Rum

Spiced rum is another name for rum liqueur, in which rum (usually golden rum, although sometime light rum and caramel coloring are used) is tinctured with a variety of spices. Our version is rich and head-turning, combining volatiles of licorice (star anise), camphor (cardamom), capsaicin (guajillo chiles), and vanillin (vanilla beans). Whereas light and golden rums are often used for mixed drinks, complex aged and spiced rums are usually served by themselves.

MAKES ABOUT 1 QUART

- 1 fifth (750 ml/3¼ cups) dark rum (80 proof)
- 20 star anise, crushed
- 20 cardamom pods, crushed
- 1 dried guajillo chile, seeded and chopped
- 2 vanilla beans (Madagascar or Bourbon), split
- ¼ cup honey

1. Combine the rum, star anise, cardamom, chile, and vanilla in a glass jar. Stir to moisten everything.

2. Seal the jar and put it in a cool, dark cabinet until the liquid is very aromatic, 1 to 2 days.

3. Strain the mixture with a mesh strainer into a clean quart jar. Do not push on the solids to extract more liquid. You should have a little more than 2¾ cups.

4. Stir in the honey.

5. Seal and store in a cool, dark cabinet. Use within 1 year.

Y *L'chaim!* *Enjoy either straight up or on the rocks.*

Tropical Orchid

This exotic blend of super-ripe mango, ginger, coconut, and vanilla (the fruit of a tropical orchid) is so exquisitely delicious that it wouldn't have to deliver anything more than sensual delight to be worthy of praise, but I'll be damned if it's not healthy to boot. Mango is high in antioxidants, especially its peel, which is included in this tincture. Coconut milk raises HDL ("good") cholesterol in the blood, and ginger helps inhibit the production of free radicals throughout the body.

MAKES ABOUT 1 QUART

1 fifth (750 ml/3¼ cups) light rum (80 proof)

1 very ripe mango, flesh and peel coarsely chopped

1 (4-inch) piece fresh ginger, minced or shredded

2 vanilla beans (Madagascar or Bourbon), split

1 cup Coconut Cream Simple Syrup (page 25)

1. Combine the rum, mango, ginger, and vanilla in a half-gallon jar. Stir to moisten everything.

2. Seal the jar and put it in a cool, dark cabinet until the liquid smells and tastes strongly of ginger and vanilla, 3 to 5 days.

3. Strain the mixture with a mesh strainer into a clean quart jar. Do not push on the solids to extract more liquid.

4. Stir in the simple syrup.

5. Seal and store in a cool, dark cabinet. Use within 1 year.

Y *Sláinte!* *As you might suspect, this liqueur makes an excellent Mango Colada (page 252).*

Nuit Noir

Licorice root, Malabar peppercorns, and Madagascar vanilla beans have little in common, except that all three are black. Black foods are relatively rare, so when three disparate ingredients come together through something as basic as black, you have to give them a whirl and see what happens. In this case, the licorice radiates flavor, the vanilla slinks in sweetly, and the pepper spanks the taste buds. This is not a monastic liqueur. Like anything that is barely self-contained, it's best to leave it alone; add a taming spritz of soda if you must.

MAKES ABOUT 1 QUART

1 fifth (750 ml/3¼ cups) vodka
  (80-100 proof)
½ cup licorice root pieces
2 tablespoons cracked black pepper
1 vanilla bean (Madagascar
  or Bourbon), split
  Big pinch of sea salt
1 cup Simple Syrup (page 24)

1. Combine the vodka, licorice root, black pepper, vanilla, and salt in a half-gallon jar. Stir to moisten everything.

2. Seal the jar and put it in a cool, dark cabinet until the liquid smells and tastes strongly of licorice, 1 to 2 days.

3. Strain the mixture with a mesh strainer into a clean quart jar. Do not push on the solids to extract more liquid.

4. Stir in the simple syrup.

5. Seal and store in a cool, dark cabinet. Use within 1 year.

Peppercorn Punch

Unrelated to Piper nigrum, Tasmanian peppercorns are the fruit of a bush in the genus Tasmannia. The peppercorn is large and some-what chewy, like a juniper berry, and its flavor is not unlike juniper blended with fennel. It has a distinctive fruitiness, some woody notes, and a few floral twinges. The sensation is complex and it really should be experienced. When soaked in alcohol, the berries turn the liquid a gorgeous deep purple hue.

MAKES ABOUT 1 QUART

1 fifth (750 ml/3¼ cups) vodka (80-100 proof)

¼ cup Tasmanian peppercorns, crushed

1 tablespoon cracked black pepper

Finely grated zest of 2 oranges

1 vanilla bean (Madagascar or Bourbon), split

1 cup Simple Syrup (page 24)

1. Combine the vodka, Tasmanian peppercorns, black pepper, orange zest, and vanilla in a half-gallon jar. Stir to moisten everything.

2. Seal the jar and put it in a cool, dark cabinet until the liquid smells and tastes strongly of pepper, 2 to 3 days.

3. Strain the mixture with a mesh strainer into a clean quart jar. Do not push on the solids to extract more liquid.

4. Stir in the simple syrup.

5. Seal and store in a cool, dark cabinet. Use within 1 year.

Y *L'chaim!* *Combine with grapefruit juice for a Greyhound with a kick.*

Forest Refuge

This blend of forest herbs, dried mushrooms, and juniper is more savory than sweet, imparting a combination of fertile, gamey aromas and a resinous, coniferous scent. The sensation is unique and surprisingly delicious. I tend to drink most herbal liqueurs on their own, but I have tried a bit of this one mixed into a peaty Scotch and it went quite well.

MAKES A LITTLE MORE THAN 1 PINT

1 fifth (750 ml/3¼ cups) Dutch-
　style gin (80 proof)
¼ cup chopped fresh rosemary
¼ cup fresh thyme leaves
¼ cup juniper berries, crushed
¼ cup dried mushrooms, such
　as porcini or morels
　Big pinch of sea salt
¼ cup Simple Syrup (page 24)

1. Combine the gin, rosemary, thyme, juniper berries, mushrooms, and salt in a half-gallon jar. Stir to moisten everything.

2. Seal the jar and put it in a cool, dark cabinet until the liquid smells and tastes strongly of herbs, 3 to 5 days.

3. Strain the mixture with a mesh strainer into a clean quart jar. Do not push on the solids to extract more liquid.

4. Stir in the simple syrup.

5. Seal and store in a cool, dark cabinet. Use within 1 year.

NUT & SEED LIQUEURS

SEEDS CREATE THE NEXT GENERATION OF PLANTS. They contain the plant embryo and a food supply (usually oil) that fuels its growth, and they are housed in an outer shell that protects the embryonic plant from outside forces. Nuts are edible seeds that are usually larger and richer in oil than other seeds; they require no cooking. All of this makes them potent flavoring agents for liqueur. All you have to do is break them open, mix them with alcohol, and wait.

There are dozens of classic nut liqueurs. Frangelico is an Italian hazelnut liqueur, Nocello is flavored with walnuts, and amaretto is made from almonds. Kahana Royale is a rich macadamia nut liqueur from Hawaii and Dumante Verdenoce is a pistachio liqueur from southern Italy. There are rum liqueurs infused with coconut, which is a very large seed.

Nut flavors are distinctive and complex, and nuttiness comprises an array of sensations, offering many delicate, almost elusive, tastes and aromas in a decidedly rich package. There are toasty roasted flavors and a protein sweetness in the same way that glistening fresh meat is sweet. Nuts and seeds are loaded with oils, an attribute that makes them unique in the vegetable world.

Most vegetables house their calories as carbohydrates, which gives them a sweet or starchy profile, but because nuts have to pack in all the energy the embryo needs to turn into a plant, carbohydrates won't do. The fat content of nuts makes them easy to toast, which brings out their characteristic flavors; many of these recipes call for the nuts to be toasted for that reason.

HOW TO USE NUTS IN LIQUEURS

Because nuts are high in oil, they can easily become rancid. Before using any nut in a liqueur recipe, smell it. If it has an off aroma, don't use it. Rancid flavors are easily absorbed into the alcohol along with all other flavors.

If you are starting with shelled walnuts, pecans, or hazelnuts, pick away all pieces of interior membrane from the walnuts or pecans, and rub the skins from toasted hazelnuts with a terrycloth towel. These skins and membranes are high in tannins, which can make your liqueur unpleasantly astringent. At the other extreme, if you are using shelled nuts, avoid salted varieties. The level of sodium will ruin the liqueur.

To toast nuts, heat a heavy skillet, preferably cast iron, over high heat for 5 minutes. Remove from the heat. Add the nuts and stir until the nuts are aromatic and lightly toasted, about 2 minutes. Dump onto a baking sheet to let cool.

Nuts can also be toasted in a microwave. Lay them out in an even single layer on a microwave-safe plate (don't cover them) and microwave at full power until the nuts are aromatic, about 3 minutes; stir halfway through.

As nut liqueurs sit, oil suspended in the alcohol can rise to the surface. Shaking the bottle for a few seconds will put the oil back in suspension. If you don't want to do that, you can set the liqueur in the freezer for a day. The oil will solidify on the surface and then can be easily skimmed away. Remember, though, the nut oils are flavorful, and they add a lightly creamy texture to the liqueur, so removing the oil will make the finished liqueur lighter and thinner.

Toasted Walnut

Copycat Nocello

Walnuts are rich in omega-3 polyunsaturated linolenic acid, making them nutritionally significant but vulnerable to rancidity. Make sure that walnuts are fresh before you buy them, either by checking a best-by date or by smelling them. If they smell bitter or acrid, do not use them for liqueur. Keep walnuts fresh by storing them in the freezer. Linolenic acid is also responsible for most of the characteristic flavor of walnuts, a combination of brown sugar, whole-wheat toast, and astringency.

MAKES ABOUT 1 QUART

1 **pound walnut pieces, broken**
1 **fifth (750 ml/3¼ cups) brandy
(80 proof)**
¼ **cup honey**
¾ **cup Brown Simple Syrup (page 24)**

1. Heat a heavy skillet, preferably cast iron, over high heat for 5 minutes. Remove from the heat. Add the walnuts and stir until the nuts are aromatic and lightly toasted, about 2 minutes. Dump onto a baking sheet and let cool until just warm to the touch, about 10 minutes.

2. Chop the nuts finely; it's easiest to use a food processor. Put the nuts into the work bowl of the processor, and chop using 3-second pulses until uniformly finely chopped, like coarse sand.

3. Combine the brandy, honey, and walnuts in a half-gallon jar. Stir to moisten everything.

4. Seal the jar and put it in a cool, dark cabinet until the liquid smells and tastes strongly of nuts, 7 to 10 days.

5. Strain the mixture with a mesh strainer into a clean quart jar. Do not push on the solids to extract more liquid. You should have about 2½ cups.

6. Stir in the simple syrup.

7. Seal and store in a cool, dark cabinet. Use within 1 year.

Y *Bottoms Up!* *Enhance a cup of coffee with a shot or invest your next Manhattan with its riches.*

Walffee

The flavor combination of sweetly roasted (light to medium) coffee and deeply toasted (to the color of lightly roasted coffee) walnuts is seamless. Bitterness, sweetness, whole wheat toast, well-done roast beef, molasses, and nuttiness embrace and reproduce, compounding one another into a new flavor altogether. Let's call it Walffee.

MAKES ABOUT 1 QUART

12 ounces walnut pieces, broken

4 ounces medium-roast coffee beans

1 fifth (750 ml/3¼ cups) brandy
(80 proof)

1 vanilla bean (Madagascar
or Bourbon), split

¼ cup molasses

1 cup Brown Simple Syrup (page 24)

1. Heat a heavy skillet, preferably cast iron, over high heat for 5 minutes. Remove from the heat. Add the walnuts and stir until the nuts are aromatic and well toasted, about 2 minutes. Stir in the coffee beans. Dump onto a baking sheet and let cool until the nuts are just warm to the touch, about 5 minutes.

2. Chop the nuts and coffee beans finely; it's easiest to use a food processor. Put the nuts and coffee beans into the work bowl of the processor, and chop using 3-second pulses until uniformly finely chopped, like coarse sand.

3. Combine the brandy, vanilla, molasses, and walnut mixture in a half-gallon jar. Stir to moisten everything.

4. Seal the jar and put it in a cool, dark cabinet until the liquid smells and tastes strongly of nuts and coffee, 7 to 10 days.

5. Strain the mixture with a mesh strainer into a clean quart jar. Do not push on the solids to extract more liquid.

6. Stir in the simple syrup.

7. Seal and store in a cool, dark cabinet. Use within 1 year.

Y *Salut!* *Spike your next espresso with a splash.*

Bitter Almond

Curiously, the flavor of domestic almonds is delicate and vaguely nutty, nothing like the blow-your-lid vibrancy of almond extract. Strong almond flavor like that is only found in wild or bitter almonds, which when chewed contain enough bitter hydrogen cyanide to kill a large dog. A byproduct of cyanide production is benzaldehyde, a fragrant molecule that is the essence of wild almond flavor and is the flavoring in almond extract; it is also found in the pits of cherries and apricots.

Bitter almonds are unavailable in the United States, but you can find apricot kernels (see Resources, page 257). Adding a few to this liqueur releases the flavor of almond without the risk of toxicity.

MAKES ABOUT 1 QUART

- **12 ounces blanched almonds**
- **4 ounces apricot kernels**
- **2½ cups vodka (80–100 proof)**
- **1 cup dry sherry (17% ABV)**
- **1¼ cups Simple Syrup (page 24)**
- **¼ teaspoon pure almond extract (optional)**

1. Chop the almonds and apricot kernels finely; it's easiest to use a food processor. Put the nuts and kernels into the work bowl of the processor, and chop using 3-second pulses until uniformly finely chopped, like coarse sand.
2. Combine the vodka, sherry, and chopped almond mixture in a half-gallon jar. Stir to moisten everything.
3. Seal the jar and put it in a cool, dark cabinet until the liquid smells and tastes strongly of bitter almond, 7 to 10 days.
4. Strain the mixture with a mesh strainer into a clean quart jar. Do not push on the solids to extract more liquid.
5. Stir in the simple syrup and extract, if desired.
6. Seal and store in a cool, dark cabinet. Use within 1 year.

Prost! *Makes a fragrant Brandy Alexander.*

Sweet Almond

Copycat Amaretto

Amaro means "bitter" in Italian; it refers to the use of bitter almonds in the production of amaretto. Although it is possible to use apricot kernels in place of California almonds to capture that wild bitter almond flavor, almond extract is more consistent and yields the same results. It is ironic that bitterness is highlighted in amaretto, because few commercial liqueurs are as cloyingly sweet. This version tames that saccharine quality, but if you like your amaretto syrupy you can add up to another ½ cup simple syrup.

MAKES ABOUT 1 QUART

1 pound blanched almonds
1 cup vodka (80–100 proof)
2 cups brandy (80 proof)
1¼ cups Simple Syrup (page 24)
2 teaspoons pure almond extract

1. Chop the nuts finely; it's easiest way to use a food processor. Put the nuts into the work bowl of the processor, and pulse in 3-second bursts until uniformly finely chopped, like coarse sand.

2. Combine the vodka, brandy, and almonds in a half-gallon jar. Stir to moisten the nuts.

3. Seal the jar and put it in a cool, dark cabinet until the liquid smells and tastes of almond, 7 to 10 days.

4. Strain the mixture with a mesh strainer into a clean quart jar. Do not push on the solids to extract more liquid.

5. Stir in the simple syrup and extract.

6. Seal and store in a cool, dark cabinet. Use within 1 year.

Y *Skål! Amaretto is a common cocktail ingredient in several popular cocktails, including the Orange-Almond Sour (page 252), the Godfather (equal parts Scotch and Amaretto), and Hawaiian Punch (page 244).*

Vanilla Almond

Is "plain vanilla" any way to characterize the second most expensive food crop in the world (saffron is the priciest)? What could be more exotic than vanilla? Each Vanilla planifolia orchid produces one exquisite bean and then dies. The flowers can be naturally pollinated only by a Melipona bee, native to Mexico.

When the French planted vanilla vines in their African colonies, the flowers would grow but would not bear fruit. Importing bees failed. The only option was to pollinate each blossom by hand, a practice that is now common for all vanilla production.

The only thing plain about vanilla is its ubiquity, which is more a testament to its versatility than to its plainness.

MAKES ABOUT 1 QUART

  1 **pound blanched almonds**
1½ **cups vodka (80–100 proof)**
1½ **cups grappa (80 proof)**
  2 **vanilla beans (Madagascar or Bourbon), split**
1¼ **cups Simple Syrup (page 24)**
 ½ **teaspoon pure almond extract (optional)**

1. Chop the nuts finely; it's easiest to use a food processor. Put the nuts into the work bowl of the processor, and chop using 3-second pulses until the nuts are uniformly finely chopped, like coarse sand.

2. Combine the vodka, grappa, almonds, and vanilla in a half-gallon jar. Stir to moisten everything.

3. Seal the jar and put it in a cool, dark cabinet until the liquid smells and tastes of vanilla and almond, 7 to 10 days.

4. Strain the mixture with a mesh strainer into a clean quart jar. Do not push on the solids to extract more liquid.

5. Stir in the simple syrup and extract, if desired.

6. Seal and store in a cool, dark cabinet. Use within 1 year.

Y *Sláinte!*   Sip with warm milk at night for an intoxicating sleep potion.

Spiced Black Walnut

Black walnuts look similar to English walnuts but have a strong, distinctive aroma that needs a worthy opponent to tame it. In this liqueur, you will find two. The first is Laphroaig, a rustic single-malt Scotch from Islay, the southernmost island of the Inner Hebrides. Islay Scotches are known for their overt smokiness, and Laphroaig is one of the smokiest. It stands up beautifully to the sharp notes of black walnut. The next is allspice, a pungent berry that is native to the Caribbean. The principal aromatic in jerk seasoning, it tastes a bit like clove, though not as strong. Together, they create a memorable liqueur.

MAKES ABOUT 1 QUART

1 cup vodka (80–100 proof)

2 cups Scotch (80 proof), preferably Laphroaig

1 pound black walnut pieces, coarsely chopped

8 allspice berries

1 cup Simple Syrup (page 24)

1. Combine the vodka, Scotch, black walnuts, and allspice berries in a half-gallon jar. Stir to moisten everything.

2. Seal the jar and put it in a cool, dark cabinet until the liquid smells and tastes strongly of black walnut, 7 to 10 days.

3. Strain the mixture with a mesh strainer into a clean quart jar. Do not push on the solids to extract more liquid.

4. Stir in the simple syrup.

5. Seal and store in a cool, dark cabinet. Use within 1 year.

Y *L'chaim!* *Use to make an unusual Manhattan.*

Chocolate Hazelnut

Nutella, the PB&J of Europe, is a testament to the nearly universal appeal of toasted hazelnuts and chocolate. It was popularized during World War II, when chocolate was in short supply in Italy. An older version, gianduia, was developed in the Alpine region of Italy when taxes on cocoa beans prompted chocolate manufacturers to cut their products with nut pastes. Today, Bottega produces a chocolate-hazelnut liqueur bearing the same name.

MAKES ABOUT 1 QUART

  1 **pound blanched hazelnuts**
1½ **cups (7½ ounces) cacao nibs**
  1 **fifth (750 ml/3¼ cups)**
      grappa (80 proof)
1¼ **cups Simple Syrup (page 24)**

1. Heat a heavy skillet, preferably cast iron, over high heat for 5 minutes. Remove from the heat. Add the hazelnuts and stir until the nuts are aromatic and lightly toasted, about 2 minutes. Dump onto a baking sheet and let cool until just warm to the touch, about 10 minutes. Rub the skins off the hazelnuts with a clean dishtowel. Stir in the cacao nibs.

2. Chop the nuts and cacao nibs finely; it's easiest to use a food processor. Put the nuts and nibs into the work bowl of the processor, and chop using 3-second pulses until uniformly finely chopped, like coarse sand.

3. Combine the grappa and hazelnut mixture in a half-gallon jar. Stir to moisten everything.

4. Seal the jar and put it in a cool, dark cabinet until the liquid smells and tastes strongly of chocolate and hazelnuts, 7 to 10 days.

5. Strain the mixture with a mesh strainer into a clean quart jar. Do not push on the solids to extract more liquid.

6. Stir in the simple syrup.

7. Seal and store in a cool, dark cabinet. Use within 1 year.

....

Ⓨ *Prost!* *Delicious in a Black or White Russian. Or make a Mocha Nut (page 240) or Chocolate-Caramel-Hazelnut Espresso (page 240).*

Toasted Hazelnut

Copycat Frangelico

Hazelnuts (a.k.a. filberts) are undistinguished when raw, a bit starchy and bitter, making their popularity seem unfounded. But when you taste them toasted, their fame pops into focus. The main aromatic compound in hazelnuts, heptanone, increases 700-fold when the nuts are toasted. The flavor of toasted hazelnuts is so vibrant that no augmentation is necessary.

MAKES ABOUT 1 QUART

1 **pound blanched hazelnuts**
1½ **cups brandy (80 proof)**
1½ **cups bourbon (80 proof)**
1 **cup Brown Simple Syrup (page 24)**

1. Heat a heavy skillet, preferably cast iron, over high heat for 5 minutes. Remove from the heat. Add the hazelnuts and stir until the nuts are aromatic and lightly toasted, about 2 minutes. Dump onto a baking sheet and let cool until just warm to the touch, about 10 minutes. Rub the skins off with a clean dishtowel.

2. Chop the nuts finely; it's easiest to use a food processor. Put the nuts into the work bowl of the processor, and chop using 3-second pulses until uniformly finely chopped, like coarse sand.

3. Combine brandy, bourbon, and hazelnuts in a half-gallon jar. Stir to moisten everything.

4. Seal the jar and put it in a cool, dark cabinet until the liquid smells and tastes strongly of hazelnuts, 7 to 10 days.

5. Strain the mixture with a mesh strainer into a clean quart jar. Do not push on the solids to extract more liquid. You should have about 2½ cups.

6. Stir in the simple syrup.

7. Seal and store in a cool, dark cabinet. Use within 1 year.

⋯⋯⋯⋯⋯⋯⋯⋯⋯⋯⋯⋯⋯⋯⋯⋯⋯⋯⋯⋯⋯⋯⋯⋯⋯⋯⋯⋯⋯⋯⋯⋯⋯

Y *Bottoms Up!* *Use this knockoff in a Mother Superior (page 253), as pictured here.*

Caramelized Chestnut

Chestnuts look like nuts in that they are large, round, and have a shell, but unlike all other nuts, chestnuts store their energy as starch rather than as oil. This gives them a mealy texture, and when they are roasted they become sweet rather than nutty. In this golden liqueur, that sweetness is underscored by infusing the chestnuts into bourbon and rum and sweetening the liqueur with caramelized sugar syrup.

MAKES ABOUT 1 QUART

24 fresh chestnuts
2 cups bourbon (80 proof)
1 cup dark rum (80 proof)
   Pinch of sea salt
1½ cups Caramelized Simple
   Syrup (page 24)

1. Preheat the oven to 375°F.

2. Cut a cross through the shell on the flat side of each chestnut, cutting through the skin beneath but not into the flesh of the nut. Put on a baking sheet, cut side up, and roast until browned and aromatic, about 35 minutes. Let cool; remove the shells and skins and chop the flesh finely.

3. Combine the bourbon, rum, chestnuts, salt, and simple syrup in a half-gallon jar. Stir to moisten everything.

4. Seal the jar and put it in a cool, dark cabinet until the liquid smells and tastes strongly of chestnuts, 7 to 10 days.

5. Strain the mixture with a mesh strainer into a clean quart jar. Do not push on the solids to extract more liquid.

6. Seal and store in a cool, dark cabinet. Use within 1 year.

Y *Sláinte!* *Mix with cream and serve over ice.*

Chocolate Coconut

In the miniaturized world of seeds, coconuts are ginormous, housing enough food to feed a developing coconut palm embryo for a whole year. Coconut meat is about 35 percent fat, on the low side for most nuts, so coconut-flavored liqueurs don't tend to separate as much as other nut liqueurs. Highly drinkable, this liqueur tastes like an Almond Joy, minus the almonds and the shreds of coconut stuck in your teeth.

MAKES ABOUT 1 QUART

1 fifth (750 ml/3¼ cups)
   light rum (80 proof)
3 cups lightly packed sweetened
   flaked coconut
1½ cups (7½ ounces) cacao nibs
½ vanilla bean (Madagascar
   or Bourbon), split
1 cup Simple Syrup (page 24)

1. Combine the rum, coconut, cacao nibs, and vanilla in a half-gallon jar. Stir to moisten everything.

2. Seal the jar and put it in a cool, dark cabinet until the liquid smells and tastes strongly of coconut and chocolate, 7 to 10 days.

3. Strain the mixture with a mesh strainer into a clean quart jar. Do not push on the solids to extract more liquid.

4. Stir in the simple syrup.

5. Seal and store in a cool, dark cabinet. Use within 1 year.

Y **Cheers!** *Substitute for chocolate liqueur in a Brandy Alexander and finish with a splash of canned coconut cream.*

Brown Sugar Pecan

Along with walnuts, pecans have a very high oil content, which, in the world of nuts, goes along with fragile texture. Pecans are easily bruised, which causes their oil to seep onto the surface, where it oxidizes and turns rancid. Always smell or taste a batch of pecans before you buy. Toasting helps bring out the nuts' sweetness and diminish rancid notes. However, once pecans are toasted, use them immediately. Like bruising, toasting encourages oil seepage, which shortens their shelf life.

MAKES ABOUT 1 QUART

1 pound pecan pieces
1 fifth (750 ml/3¼ cups)
   dark rum (80 proof)
   Finely grated zest of 1 orange
1¼ cups Brown Simple Syrup (page 24)

1. Heat a heavy skillet, preferably cast iron, over high heat for 5 minutes. Remove from the heat. Add the pecans and stir until the nuts are aromatic and lightly toasted, about 2 minutes. Dump onto a baking sheet and let cool until just warm to the touch, about 10 minutes.

2. Chop the nuts finely; it's easiest to use a food processor. Put the nuts into the work bowl of the processor, and chop using 3-second pulses until uniformly finely chopped, like coarse sand.

3. Combine the rum, pecans, and orange zest in a half-gallon jar. Stir to moisten everything.

4. Seal the jar and put it in a cool, dark cabinet until the liquid smells and tastes strongly of nuts, 7 to 10 days.

5. Strain the mixture with a mesh strainer into a clean quart jar. Do not push on the solids to extract more liquid.

6. Stir in the simple syrup.

7. Seal and store in a cool, dark cabinet. Use within 1 year.

Y *Santé!* *An elegant addition to nearly any bourbon- or rum-based cocktail.*

Caramel Candy

Copycat Praline-Pecan Liqueur

Cooks have been coating nuts with candy since the seventeenth century, and pralines — almonds coated in caramelized sugar — were one of the earliest types. The inspiration for this caramel-nut liqueur is Southern pralines, which are made from untoasted pecans stuck into a puddle of caramel-flavored fudge. With no roasting or toasting, this nut-based recipe is particularly quick and easy. The result is sweet and savory, a delicious spike to warm apple cider or an easy way to gussy up a glass of bourbon.

MAKES ABOUT 1 QUART

1 **pound pecan pieces**
1 **fifth (750 ml/3¼ cups) bourbon (80 proof)**
1 **vanilla bean (Madagascar or Bourbon), split**
   Pinch of fine sea salt
1 **cup Caramelized Simple Syrup (page 24)**

1. Chop the nuts finely; it's easiest to use a food processor. Put the nuts into the work bowl of the processor, and chop using 3-second pulses until uniformly finely chopped, like coarse sand.

2. Combine the bourbon, pecans, vanilla, salt, and simple syrup in a half-gallon jar. Stir to moisten everything.

3. Seal the jar and put it in a cool, dark cabinet until the liquid smells and tastes strongly of pecans, 7 to 10 days.

4. Strain the mixture with a mesh strainer into a clean quart jar. Do not push on the solids to extract more liquid.

5. Seal and store in a cool, dark cabinet. Use within 1 year.

Y *Salut!* *Try a Glazed Wild Turkey (page 246).*

Honey Pistachio

A relative of the cashew, but slightly oiler and much more flavorful, the pistachio is unique in nutdom for being green when ripe. The color comes from chlorophyll, which stays bright if the pistachios are handled in a way that preserves the pigment. They must be grown in a relatively cool climate, and they must be picked while still slightly immature. The nuts are then roasted at low temperatures to keep them from browning, which would cause their color to fade.

Although pistachio liqueurs are frequently dyed green, I have found that a good amount of chlorophyll enters the alcohol during tincturing, yielding a beautiful, soft, and natural tint.

MAKES ABOUT 1 QUART

12 ounces shelled pistachio nuts
1½ cups vodka (80-100 proof)
1½ cups dry vermouth (18% ABV)
 Finely grated zest of 1 lemon
1 cup honey

1. Chop the nuts finely; it's easiest to use a food processor. Put the nuts into the work bowl of the processor, and chop using 3-second pulses until uniformly finely chopped, like coarse sand.

2. Combine the vodka, pistachios, vermouth, lemon zest, and honey in a half-gallon jar. Stir to moisten everything.

3. Seal the jar and put it in a cool, dark cabinet until the liquid smells and tastes strongly of pistachios, 7 to 10 days.

4. Strain the mixture with a mesh strainer into a clean quart jar. Do not push on the solids to extract more liquid.

5. Seal and store in a cool, dark cabinet. Use within 1 year.

Y *Cheers!* *Makes a sophisticated stand-in for amaretto and is delicious drizzled over ice cream.*

Open Sesame

The process for making sesame liqueur is almost identical to the process for making Black Poppy (page 149), except that sesame seeds must be toasted to enrich their flavor. They have a similarly high oil content to poppy seeds and yield a liqueur that is equally rich. The main difference is the flavor. Sesame seeds are decidedly nutty (high in protein), while poppy seeds tend to be more acrid (high in alkaloids) before they are sweetened. Although sesame seeds come in a wide variety of colors, paler seeds have a better flavor for making liqueur and yield better color after toasting. Sesame liqueur mixes well with orange, ginger, and coconut flavors when making mixed drinks.

MAKES A SCANT FIFTH

1 pound white sesame seeds,
    about 3 cups
1 fifth (750 ml/3¼ cups)
    vodka (80-100 proof)
1 (1-inch) piece fresh ginger, finely grated
½ cup honey
1 cup Simple Syrup (page 24)

1. Heat a heavy skillet, preferably cast iron, over high heat for 5 minutes. Remove from the heat. Add the sesame seeds and stir until aromatic and lightly toasted, about 1 minute. Dump onto a baking sheet and let cool until just warm to the touch, about 10 minutes.

2. Combine the vodka, sesame seeds, ginger, and honey in a half-gallon jar. Stir to moisten everything.

3. Seal the jar and put it in a cool, dark cabinet until the liquid smells and tastes strongly of sesame and ginger, 7 to 10 days.

4. Strain the mixture with a mesh strainer into a clean quart jar. Do not push on the solids to extract more liquid. You should have about 2½ cups.

5. Stir in the simple syrup.

6. Seal and store in a cool, dark cabinet. Use within 1 year.

Y *Santé!* *Substitute for fruit liqueur in a Mai Tai or a Cosmopolitan.*

Rosemary Pignoli

Pine nuts are harvested from about a dozen different types of pines, most commonly in Asia (Korea and China), the southwestern United States, and Italy. Each type has its own shape and size, and most important for our purposes, different fat contents. Italian pignoli are the leanest and most expensive but the best for making liqueur; the others will precipitate an oil slick on the surface of the finished liqueur.

Staying in the Italian style, the liqueur is flavored with rosemary, orange, and a hint of vanilla. Sugar is kept low to allow the resinous piney qualities to shine through.

MAKES ABOUT 1 QUART

1 pound Italian pine nuts
1 fifth (750 ml/3¼ cups) vodka (80–100 proof)
2 fresh rosemary sprigs
¼ vanilla bean (Madagascar or Bourbon), split
  Finely grated zest of 1 orange
¾ cup Simple Syrup (page 24)

1. Heat a heavy skillet, preferably cast iron, over high heat for 5 minutes. Remove from the heat. Add the pine nuts and stir until the nuts are aromatic and lightly toasted, about 1 minute. Dump onto a baking sheet and let cool until just warm to the touch, about 10 minutes.

2. Chop the nuts finely; it's easiest to use a food processor. Put the nuts into the work bowl of the processor, and chop using 3-second pulses until uniformly finely chopped, like coarse sand.

3. Combine the vodka, chopped pine nuts, rosemary, vanilla, and orange zest in a half-gallon jar. Stir to moisten everything.

4. Seal the jar and put it in a cool, dark cabinet until the liquid smells and tastes strongly of rosemary and orange, and subtly piney, 7 to 10 days.

5. Strain the mixture with a mesh strainer into a clean quart jar. Do not push on the solids to extract more liquid.

6. Stir in the simple syrup.

7. Seal and store in a cool, dark cabinet. Use within 1 year.

Y *Skål!* *Serve simply over rocks or use in a glaze for roasted chicken or pork.*

Toasted Tropics

Mild and fatty, macadamias and coconuts are unlike other tree nuts. Truly tropical, they are low in pungent tannins and alkaloids. Both have exceedingly hard shells and, particularly in the case of macadamias, are almost exclusively sold already shelled. The macadamia has the added distinction of having the highest fat content of any nut grown commercially, a whopping 72 percent (mostly monounsaturated). In this exotic liqueur the nuts are toasted, which improves their flavor immeasurably.

MAKES ABOUT 1 QUART

12 ounces blanched macadamia nuts

8 ounces lightly packed sweetened flaked coconut (2⅔ cups)

1 fifth (750 ml/3¼ cups) light rum (80 proof)

Finely grated zest of 2 limes

1 cup Simple Syrup (page 24)

1. Heat a heavy skillet, preferably cast iron, over high heat for 5 minutes. Remove from the heat. Add the macadamias and coconut and stir until the nuts are aromatic and the nuts and coconut are lightly toasted, about 2 minutes. Dump onto a baking sheet and let cool until just warm to the touch, about 10 minutes.

2. Chop the nuts and coconut finely; it's easiest to use a food processor. Put the mixture into the work bowl of the processor, and chop using 3-second pulses until crumbly.

3. Combine the rum, nut mixture, and lime zest in a half-gallon jar. Stir to moisten everything.

4. Seal the jar and put it in a cool, dark cabinet until the liquid smells and tastes strongly of nuts and coconut, 7 to 10 days.

5. Strain the mixture with a mesh strainer into a clean quart jar. Do not push on the solids to extract more liquid.

6. Stir in the simple syrup.

7. Seal and store in a cool, dark cabinet. Use within 1 year.

Y **Bottoms Up!** *Use this liqueur to spike a Hawaiian Mojito (page 244) or a Cola Coffee (page 243).*

Black Poppy

There are one to two million poppy seeds in a pound, give or take a couple of thousand (3,300 in a gram). The flavor is oily and complex and the color a beautiful blue-black. Unfortunately for making liqueur, that color is an illusion. The outside pigment layer is brown but is covered with calcium oxalate crystals, which refract light in such a way that the selected wavelengths appear blue. When tinctured, the crystals disappear and the brown pigment comes through. In spite of the less attractive color, this liquor has a savory flavor and rich consistency.

MAKES ABOUT 1 QUART

12 ounces poppy seeds, about 3 cups
 1 fifth (750 ml/3¼ cups)
    golden rum (80 proof)
 1 vanilla bean (Madagascar
    or Bourbon), split
 1 cup Simple Syrup (page 24)

1. Grind the poppy seeds in batches in a small spice grinder into a grainy paste.

2. Combine the rum, poppy seeds, and vanilla a quart jar. Stir to moisten everything.

3. Seal the jar and put it in a cool, dark cabinet until the liquid smells and tastes strongly of poppy seeds, 7 to 10 days.

4. Strain the mixture with a fine-mesh strainer into a clean quart jar. Do not push on the solids to extract more liquid.

5. Stir in the simple syrup.

6. Seal and store in a cool, dark cabinet. Use within 1 year.

Ⓨ *L'chaim!* *Poppy seed liqueur is best served simply over ice.*

FLORAL LIQUEURS

THE PURPOSE OF A FLOWER IS SINGULAR AND ITS LIFE IS FLEETING — it exists to attract pollinators with its seductive scent or scintillating color or both. Once that task is complete, the scent subsides, the color fades, and the blossom shrivels and dies.

Although all parts of edible flowers are edible, the petals (corolla) are the main source of volatile chemical aromas and pigments, so it is largely the corolla that is used for liqueur making. The main exception is saffron, which is the stigma (the pollen-holding part) of a crocus.

Although fresh flower petals are readily available from your garden or party stores and websites that sell them for tossing at weddings, dried petals are preferred for tincturing. Their perfumes and colors have been stabilized, so they yield more consistent results, and the volatile elements are concentrated, so a little bit goes a long way.

Dried petals are available online and in specialty stores (see Resources, page 257). Drying flowers is not difficult, but you need a few days with relatively low humidity. Tie freshly picked flowers into bouquets and hang upside down in a dark, dry, well-ventilated area. Depending on the size and type of flower, drying will take anywhere from 24 to 96 hours. When the petals feel dry but not brittle, store them in an airtight container for 2 to 3 months.

I CAN EAT YOU, I CAN EAT YOU NOT

When making flower-infused liqueurs, only use flowers that are edible to begin with. Soaking poisonous blooms in alcohol doesn't make them any less toxic.

EDIBLE FLOWERS		INEDIBLE FLOWERS	
Angelica	Jasmine	Anemone	Oleander
Chamomile	Lavender	Buttercup	Poinsettia
Daylily	Lilac	Columbine	Privet
Elderflower	Linden	Daffodil	Rhododendron
Fruit blossoms	Marigold	Foxglove	Sweet Pea
Geraniums	Nasturtium	Hydrangea	Wisteria
Hibiscus	Pansy	Iris	
Honeysuckle	Rose	Lily of the Valley	
Hops	Violet	Narcissus	

Lavender Harmony

Lavender is well known for its powers of relaxation, hence its inclusion in sachets, massage oil, and bath soap. It also is a classic culinary herb, highlighting scores of dishes flavored with herbes de Provence. This simple aromatic dram takes its inspiration from both attributes, amending lavender's delicate floral perfume and light flavor with the herb and fruit scents in Dutch-style gin. The lighter lavender notes are strengthened with a bass chord of vanilla, plus some honey for harmony.

MAKES ABOUT 1 QUART

1 fifth (750 ml/3¼ cups) Dutch-style gin (80 proof)
1 ounce (about 2½ cups) dried lavender blossoms
1 vanilla bean (Madagascar or Bourbon), split
1 cup honey

1. Combine the gin, lavender, vanilla, and honey in a half-gallon jar. Stir to moisten everything.

2. Seal the jar and put it in a cool, dark cabinet until the liquid smells and tastes strongly of lavender, 3 to 5 days.

3. Strain the mixture with a mesh strainer into a clean quart jar. Do not push on the solids to extract more liquid.

4. Seal and store in a cool, dark cabinet. Use within 1 year.

Y *Skål! Use in place of vermouth in a bourbon Manhattan or mix up some Blue Lavender (page 254).*

Lavender White Tea

White tea is quite cool. Comprising both the buds and leaves of the tea plant, it has a floral quality that is unique among teas, making it a natural partner to other floral flavors. When brewed, the resulting tea is closer to pale gold; its name comes from silvery hairs on the unopened buds that give the tea leaves a whitish cast.

The botanicals are minimally processed, being dried only enough to wither the buds and leaves. The leaves are not allowed to ferment as they are in the production of black and oolong teas. White tea contains high levels of catechins, which help to reduce the occurrence of the atherosclerotic plaques associated with stroke and coronary thrombosis.

MAKES ABOUT 1 QUART

1 cup vodka (80–100 proof)

2 cups dry vermouth (18% ABV)

1 ounce (about 1 cup) white tea leaves

1 ounce (about 2½ cups) dried lavender blossoms

1 cup Simple Syrup (page 24)

1. Combine the vodka, vermouth, white tea, and lavender in a half-gallon jar. Stir to moisten everything.

2. Seal the jar and put it in a cool, dark cabinet until the liquid smells and tastes strongly of lavender, 3 to 5 days.

3. Strain the mixture with a mesh strainer into a clean quart jar. Do not push on the solids to extract more liquid.

4. Stir in the simple syrup.

5. Seal and store in a cool, dark cabinet. Use within 1 year.

Y **Sláinte!** *A natural for spiking an iced tea or mixing with lemon-lime soda over ice.*

Honeysuckle Honey

In this simple liqueur, dried honeysuckle blossoms are infused into brandy that has been gilded with a bit of honey. Deceptively innocent and decidedly scrumptious, the booze glows like amber and smells like a summer evening. You can employ it wherever you would normally add sweet vermouth, add it to a steaming cup of herbal tea, or just sip it unadorned, speakeasy style, from a demitasse.

MAKES ABOUT 1 QUART

1 fifth (750 ml/3¼ cups) brandy
  (80 proof)
1 ounce (about 2½ cups) dried
  honeysuckle flowers
1 cup honey

1. Combine the brandy, honeysuckle, and honey in a half-gallon jar. Stir to moisten everything.

2. Seal the jar and put it in a cool, dark cabinet until the liquid smells and tastes strongly of honey, 3 to 5 days.

3. Strain the mixture with a mesh strainer into a clean quart jar. Do not push on the solids to extract more liquid.

4. Seal and store in a cool, dark cabinet. Use within 1 year.

Rose-Sauternes Cordial

The boudoir scent of dried rose petals is matched sublimely by Sauternes, a wine that is distinctive for being made from fruit that has been affected by Botrytis cinerea, a.k.a. noble rot. The grapes shrivel on the vine, turning partially into raisins, which results in a concentrated sweetness and intensely perfumed wine. The combo is enough to cause a statue to swoon.

MAKES ABOUT 1 QUART

2   cups Sauternes (15% ABV)
1   cup vodka (80-100 proof)
1   ounce (about 2½ cups) dried rose petals
1   cup Simple Syrup (page 24)

1. Combine the Sauternes, vodka, and rose petals in a half-gallon jar. Stir to moisten everything.

2. Seal the jar and put it in a cool, dark cabinet until the liquid smells and tastes strongly of roses, 3 to 5 days.

3. Strain the mixture with a mesh strainer into a clean quart jar. Do not push on the solids to extract more liquid.

4. Stir in the simple syrup.

5. Seal and store in a cool, dark cabinet. Use within 1 year.

Y *Salut!* *Serve at room temperature or ever so slightly cooler in small stemware. In the summer it makes a seductive spritzer.*

Raspberry Rose

Rose perfume is blousy and bold and tricky to tame. Raspberry, with its lush flavor and bright color, is a worthy companion. Usually I would expect and even encourage a potent flavor like rose to have its way, but when I introduced these two, I was shocked at how graciously the rose slipped into the background, creating a delightfully ethereal fruit liqueur. It makes an enchanting cooler poured over ice and splashed with soda.

MAKES ABOUT 1 QUART

1 **fifth (750 ml/3¼ cups) vodka (80-100 proof)**

1 **ounce (about 2½ cups) dried rose petals**

1 **cup fresh raspberries**
  Finely grated zest of 1 tangerine

1 **cup Simple Syrup (page 24)**

1. Combine the vodka, rose petals, raspberries, and tangerine zest in a half-gallon jar. Stir to moisten everything.

2. Seal the jar and put it in a cool, dark cabinet until the liquid smells and tastes strongly of roses, 3 to 5 days.

3. Strain the mixture with a mesh strainer into a clean quart jar. Do not push on the solids to extract more liquid.

4. Stir in the simple syrup.

5. Seal and store in a cool, dark cabinet. Use within 1 year.

Y *Prost!* Try some Electric Raspberry Lemonade, shown here (page 243).

Chamomile Angel

Chamomile is calming, angelica promotes digestion and boosts the immune system, and tarragon is rich in antioxidants that reduce inflammation throughout the body. If your body is a temple, these three are its guardian angels. The flavor of this liqueur is multidimensional — floral, herbal, and bittersweet. Angelica has a stimulating bitter aftertaste (indicative of digestive aids) that works seamlessly with the aromatics and sugar syrup.

MAKES ABOUT 1 QUART

2 cups Dutch-style gin (80 proof)

1 cup dry vermouth (18% ABV)

1 ounce (about 2½ cups) dried chamomile blossoms

½ cup chopped dried angelica root

3 tablespoons dried tarragon

1 cup Simple Syrup (page 24)

1. Combine the gin, vermouth, chamomile, angelica, and tarragon in a half-gallon jar. Stir to moisten everything.

2. Seal the jar and put it in a cool, dark cabinet until the liquid smells and tastes strongly of herbs, 3 to 5 days.

3. Strain the mixture with a mesh strainer into a clean quart jar. Do not push on the solids to extract more liquid.

4. Stir in the simple syrup.

5. Seal and store in a cool, dark cabinet. Use within 1 year.

Y **Cheers!** *Mix with tonic water for an excellent Tummy Tamer (page 256).*

Pure Gold

Calendula (marigold) is one of those floral herbs whose health benefits seem to have no bounds. It is good for disease prevention and helps relieve inflammation, menstrual cramps, and tummy aches. In addition, it has a glorious golden color, which it effortlessly shares with this gorgeous liqueur. The gold is enhanced by saffron threads, the crimson stigmas of the saffron crocus. Though beautiful, neither saffron nor marigold has a distinctive aroma, so the principal flavor in this liqueur comes from orange zest.

MAKES ABOUT 1 QUART

1 fifth (750 ml/3¼ cups) vodka (80–100 proof)
1 ounce (about 2½ cups) dried calendula (marigold) flowers
1 tablespoon saffron threads
   Finely grated zest of 6 oranges
1 cup Simple Syrup (page 24)

1. Combine the vodka, calendula, saffron, and orange zest in a half-gallon jar. Stir to moisten everything.

2. Seal the jar and put it in a cool, dark cabinet until the liquid is golden and smells and tastes strongly of orange, 3 to 5 days.

3. Strain the mixture with a mesh strainer into a clean quart jar. Do not push on the solids to extract more liquid. Return a few threads of the saffron to the liquid for panache.

4. Stir in the simple syrup.

5. Seal and store in a cool, dark cabinet. Use within 1 year.

Y *Santé!* *Makes a vibrant Sunshine Cosmo (page 248) and an iridescent Screwdriver.*

Hibiscus Citrus

Glowing red and fragrantly tart, hibiscus blends effortlessly with citrus flavors. Red hibiscus is associated with the Hindu goddess Kali, consort of Shiva, the god of eternal time. Ironic because hibiscus blossoms are notoriously fragile, wilting within hours of harvesting, but that's all the more reason to capture their vibrant color and delicious medicinal tang through drying. Hibiscus blooms are high in vitamin C, and in some medical studies have been shown to lower blood pressure.

MAKES ABOUT 1 QUART

1 **fifth (750 ml/3¼ cups) vodka (80-100 proof)**
1 **ounce (about 2½ cups) dried hibiscus flowers (see Resources)**
   Finely grated zest of 1 lemon
   Finely grated zest of 1 lime
   Finely grated zest of 1 orange
1 **cup Simple Syrup (page 24)**

1. Combine the vodka, hibiscus, lemon zest, lime zest, and orange zest in a half-gallon jar. Stir to moisten everything.

2. Seal the jar and put it in a cool, dark cabinet until the liquid smells and tastes strongly of citrus, 3 to 5 days.

3. Strain the mixture with a mesh strainer into a clean quart jar. Do not push on the solids to extract more liquid.

4. Stir in the simple syrup.

5. Seal and store in a cool, dark cabinet. Use within 1 year.

Y *Bottoms Up!* Use in place of traditional Sour mix.

Ruby Slippers

Hibiscus and rose live at opposite corners of the flavor spectrum, but in color they are utterly simpatico. The taste of hibiscus is sharp and bright (about 25 percent organic acids by weight), while rose is soft and welcoming (geraniol, its prime aromatic molecule, is generically fruity and is used in the production of imitation fruit flavors like peach, raspberry, pineapple, and watermelon). Opposites attract, however, and together these two are damned near all-encompassing. The color of this liqueur, a crystalline ruby glow, is breathtaking.

MAKES ABOUT 1 QUART

1 fifth (750 ml/3¼ cups) vodka
   (80-100 proof)
1 ounce (about 2½ cups) dried
   hibiscus flowers (see Resources)
1 ounce (about 2½ cups)
   dried red rose petals
1 tablespoon dried tarragon
1 cup Simple Syrup (page 24)

1. Combine the vodka, hibiscus, rose petals, and tarragon in a half-gallon jar. Stir to moisten everything.

2. Seal the jar and put it in a cool, dark cabinet until the liquid smells and tastes strongly of flowers, 3 to 5 days.

3. Strain the mixture with a mesh strainer into a clean quart jar. Do not push on the solids to extract more liquid.

4. Stir in the simple syrup.

5. Seal and store in a cool, dark cabinet. Use within 1 year.

Y *Salut!* *Flavor a Daiquiri or a Margarita or make a sexy Blushing Spritzer (page 243).*

Orange Blossom

The pervasive scent of orange blossoms on a tree vanishes as soon as the blooms are plucked, so to capture their heady allure in a liqueur I was forced to reinvent nature. Jasmine has an all-purpose floral perfume that survives drying beautifully. When combined with orange peel (bursting with fragrant orange oils) they imitate the scent of orange flowers. Real orange blossoms are more delicate, but not more delicious.

MAKES ABOUT 1 QUART

1½ cups vodka (80-100 proof)
1 cup dry vermouth (18% ABV)
1 ounce (about 2½ cups) dried jasmine or honeysuckle flowers
Finely grated zest of 3 oranges
1 cup Simple Syrup (page 24)

1. Combine the vodka, vermouth, jasmine, and orange zest in a half-gallon jar. Stir to moisten everything.

2. Seal the jar and put it in a cool, dark cabinet until the liquid smells and tastes strongly of oranges and flowers, 3 to 5 days.

3. Strain the mixture with a mesh strainer into a clean quart jar. Do not push on the solids to extract more liquid.

4. Stir in the simple syrup.

5. Seal and store in a cool, dark cabinet. Use within 1 year.

....

Y *Prost!* *Use to perfume a simple Screwdriver or make an Orange Blossom Mimosa (page 244).*

Hop Blossom

I find most bourbons pedestrian — nice enough, but a little too sweet and often unfortunately flabby (give me rye any day). So when confronted with a bourbon shot, I rely on a drop of bitters to perk things up. That's the idea here. By infusing bourbon with hops (the bittering blossom common to beer) and a pinch of cinchona (bitter quinine flavor), you achieve a bourbon with cojones. It's a perfect base for Manhattans and Old-Fashioneds; no further bitters necessary.

MAKES ABOUT 1 QUART

2½ cups bourbon (80 proof)
⅛ ounce (½ cup) hops blossoms
2 teaspoons cinchona powder
   Finely grated zest of 4 oranges
1 cup Simple Syrup (page 24)

1. Combine the bourbon, hops, cinchona, and orange zest in a half-gallon jar. Stir to moisten everything.

2. Seal the jar and put it in a cool, dark cabinet until the liquid smells and tastes strongly of hops, 3 to 5 days.

3. Strain the mixture with a mesh strainer into a clean quart jar. Do not push on the solids to extract more liquid.

4. Stir in the simple syrup.

5. Seal and store in a cool, dark cabinet. Use within 1 year.

🍸 *Skål!* *Some variations on a theme: Manhattan Streamlined (page 246), New-Fashioned Old-Fashioned (page 249), and Black Velvet Redux (page 254).*

Elderflower Blush

Copycat St-Germain

St-Germain, a tropically sweet herbal-floral French liqueur made from wild elderflowers hand-harvested in the French Alps, comes in a breathtakingly elegant bottle. Archly tapered and fluted like an Art Nouveau column, it is the classiest package on the barroom wall. I have tried my best to match its beauty, and though I still like the original better, this copycat version is delicious in its own right and far less expensive per bottle. Use it in place of vermouth in a Martini or wherever else you like to use vermouth.

MAKES ABOUT 1 QUART

2 cups vodka (80-100 proof)

1 cup dry vermouth (18% ABV)

1 ounce (about 2½ cups) dried elderflower blossoms

3 Bartlett pears, seeded, stemmed, and chopped

Pulp from 1 passion fruit

Finely grated zest of ½ lemon

1¼ cups Simple Syrup (page 24)

1. Combine the vodka, vermouth, elderflowers, pears, passion fruit, and lemon zest in a half-gallon jar. Stir to moisten everything.

2. Seal the jar and put it in a cool, dark cabinet until the liquid smells and tastes strongly of flowers and fruit, 7 to 10 days.

3. Strain the mixture with a mesh strainer into a clean quart jar. Do not push on the solids to extract more liquid.

4. Stir in the simple syrup.

5. Seal and store in a cool, dark cabinet. Use within 1 year.

....

Y *L'chaim!* *Sit in the garden sipping a Flowering Martini, pictured (page 248), or Kiwi Flower Crush (page 250).*

COFFEE, TEA & CHOCOLATE LIQUEURS

CHOCOLATE IS A FOOD SET APART. Too much sugar is cloying. Too much cayenne burns. But too much chocolate is an oxymoron. So it is only fitting to find another way to consume our favorite decadence.

Chocolate liqueurs are some of the easiest to like, with coffee running a close second, and because both flavors are readily available, they are some of the easiest liqueurs to tincture.

I have also included a few tea liqueurs in this chapter, partially because it is a common hot beverage, like coffee and chocolate, but also because tea leaves, like cocoa and coffee beans, are almost always fermented. Fermentation enriches the flavors of raw produce. Just as it changes grapes into wine, and barley into beer, it transforms the fruit of the *Theobroma cacao* tree and the *Coffea* bush, and the dried leaves of *Camellia sinesis,* into super-rich commodities that are three of the most valuable agricultural products in the world.

Tea liqueurs are more subtle than coffee and chocolate varieties, closer in flavor to herbal and floral recipes, but they have an interesting grown-up astringency that makes them highly appropriate for this group.

For most chocolate liqueurs I use cacao nibs. Nothing more than cracked cocoa beans that have been fermented and roasted, nibs contain all of the flavor and fatty elements of the cocoa beans. They produce beautifully colored transparent chocolate liqueurs that are free of sediment and full of flavor.

For coffee I try to use recently roasted beans that I crack right before adding to the alcohol. As with cacao nibs, cracking the beans rather than grinding them keeps sediment to a minimum. Put the beans in a ziplock bag, seal it, and pound them with a rubber mallet. Use any roast you prefer, but dark-roast coffees have less perfume and more bitterness than lighter roasts.

In the early stages of roasting coffee beans, carbs are broken down into various acids that give light brown beans a pronounced tartness. As roasting proceeds, the acids are replaced by bitter compounds, and the distinctive aromas that distinguish high-quality beans are overshadowed by more generic roasted flavors.

For liqueurs with an espresso flavor, that dark-roast jolt is what you are looking for, but when you want a more nuanced coffee flavor, choose light- to medium-roast beans.

Whole loose tea leaves deliver the freshest flavor and cleanest tincture for tea liqueurs, but tea bags are fine if that's all you have. White and green teas are less tannic than longer-fermented oolong and black teas and will yield a milder, more perfumed liqueur. Black teas possess a generic astringent quality that acts as a foil to sweetness in a liqueur, bitters in a cocktail.

Double Shot

Copycat Kahlúa or Tia Maria

Supercharged coffee liqueur lies at the fulcrum of perfect energy balance, weighing the neuron-stimulating potency of caffeine against the soporific effect of alcohol. The coffee is administered on two fronts — cracked dark-roast beans are infused into the alcohol, and brewed coffee is used as the base for the sugar syrup. Use this in any drink that calls for a standard coffee liqueur, like a Black Russian or an Irish Coffee.

MAKES ABOUT 1 QUART

 1 **fifth (750 ml/3¼ cups) vodka (80-100 proof)**
1½ **cups (7½ ounces) dark-roast coffee beans, cracked**
 Finely grated zest of 1 lemon
 ¾ **cup brewed espresso**
 ¾ **cup sugar**

1. Combine the vodka, coffee beans, and lemon zest in a half-gallon jar. Stir to moisten everything.

2. Seal the jar and put it in a cool, dark cabinet until the liquid smells and tastes strongly of coffee, 3 to 5 days.

3. While the liqueur is maturing, make coffee-flavored syrup by combining the brewed espresso and sugar in a small saucepan. Heat over medium heat until the mixture turns translucent and bubbles form around the edge. Do not allow the mixture to boil.

4. Strain the mixture with a mesh strainer into a clean quart jar. Do not push on the solids to extract more liquid.

5. Stir in the coffee syrup.

6. Seal and store in a cool, dark cabinet. Use within 1 year.

Y *Cheers!* Wake up with a B-52 (page 239) or Cola Coffee (page 243).

Viennese Jo

Coffee is serious business on the Danube. Coffeehouse menus typically describe no fewer than two dozen coffees, each with its own garnish and plate service. Several are served with shots of liqueur. Viennese Jo is inspired by the Pharisäer served at Vienna's Café Central in the Innere Stadt — black coffee served with whipped cream on the side, a small glass of rum, and a chaser of ice water. You have a choice of cinnamon or cocoa sprinkled on top. Because the cream would separate as the liqueur ages, it has to be added as you serve it.

MAKES ABOUT 1 QUART

1 fifth (750 ml/3¼ cups)
  light rum (80 proof)
1½ cups (7½ ounces) medium-roast
  coffee beans, cracked
3 cinnamon sticks, cracked
1¼ cups Simple Syrup (page 24)

1. Combine the rum, coffee beans, and cinnamon in a half-gallon jar. Stir to moisten everything.

2. Seal the jar and put it in a cool, dark cabinet until the liquid smells and tastes strongly of coffee, 3 to 5 days.

3. Strain the mixture with a mesh strainer into a clean quart jar. Do not push on the solids to extract more liquid.

4. Stir in the simple syrup.

5. Seal and store in a cool, dark cabinet. Use within 1 year.

Y *Santé!* A teaspoon or two of cream for every 2 ounces of liqueur is sufficient.

Latte Liqueur

A caffe latte should have about a 1:3 coffee-to-milk ratio. The coffee should be espresso, the milk should be steamed, and the whole should be topped with a spoonful of milk foam. Cinnamon is optional. Since it is impossible to simulate the layering effect of milk foam in a liqueur, and since steamed milk will limit the life of the bottle, the best solution is to use condensed milk, which adds the necessary sweetness and is stable enough to be used in a tincture.

MAKES ABOUT 1 QUART

1 fifth (750 ml/3¼ cups) brandy (80 proof)

1½ cups (7½ ounces) dark-roast coffee beans, cracked

1 cinnamon stick, cracked

1 (14-ounce) can sweetened condensed milk

1. Combine the brandy, coffee beans, and cinnamon in a half-gallon jar. Stir to moisten everything.

2. Seal the jar and put it in a cool, dark cabinet until the liquid smells and tastes strongly of coffee, 3 to 5 days.

3. Strain the mixture with a mesh strainer into a clean quart jar. Do not push on the solids to extract more liquid.

4. Stir in the condensed milk.

5. Seal and store in the refrigerator. Use within 2 months.

Y *Salut!* In winter, use Latte Liqueur to spike your evening cocoa.

Café NOLA

Café brûlot is a New Orleans classic. Brûlot, meaning "burnt" in French, refers to the practice of flaming a pan of orange peel, clove, cinnamon, brandy, coffee, and melted sugar. While the flames flare, you raise the spiral of orange peel on the prongs of a fork and ladle the flaming coffee down the spiral. The presentation and the flavors are memorable, and here they are forged forever in an orange-coffee liqueur that is much less labor-intensive than the flaming original.

MAKES ABOUT 1 QUART

1   fifth (750 ml/3¼ cups) brandy
      (80 proof)
1   cup (4 ounces) medium-roast
      coffee beans, cracked
      Finely grated zest of 2 oranges
3   whole cloves
1   cinnamon stick, cracked
1¼ cups Caramelized Simple
      Syrup (page 24)

1. Combine the brandy, coffee beans, orange zest, cloves, and cinnamon in a half-gallon jar. Stir to moisten everything.

2. Seal the jar and put it in a cool, dark cabinet until the liquid smells and tastes strongly of coffee, 3 to 5 days.

3. Strain the mixture with a mesh strainer into a clean quart jar. Do not push on the solids to extract more liquid.

4. Stir in the simple syrup.

5. Seal and store in a cool, dark cabinet. Use within 1 year.

Y *Skål!* *Serve warm and unadorned in demitasse cups.*

Coffee Nut

I am not a fan of flavored coffees, but hazelnut coffee at least makes some sense to me. The sweet nuttiness of toasted hazelnuts masks some of the coffee's natural bitterness without completely changing the flavor profile. Nuts and beans have protein flavors in common. And the method used here to integrate hazelnut nuance into the coffee is more natural than the technique used for flavoring roasted coffee beans, which is largely done with chemical solvents.

MAKES ABOUT 1 QUART

1 fifth (750 ml/3¼ cups) vodka
   (80–100 proof)
1 cup (4 ounces) medium-roast
   coffee beans, cracked
½ cup (3 ounces) roasted
   hazelnuts, finely ground
1 vanilla bean (Madagascar
   or Bourbon), split
1 cup Brown Simple Syrup (page 24)
¼ cup honey

1. Combine the vodka, coffee beans, hazelnuts, and vanilla in a half-gallon jar. Stir to moisten everything.

2. Seal the jar and put it in a cool, dark cabinet until the liquid smells and tastes strongly of coffee, 3 to 5 days.

3. Strain the mixture with a mesh strainer into a clean quart jar. Do not push on the solids to extract more liquid.

4. Stir in the simple syrup and honey.

5. Seal and store in a cool, dark cabinet. Use within 1 year.

Y *Cheers!* *Make a Hazelnut Coffee (page 240) by adding a splash of Coffee Nut to a hot cup of java.*

MOCA

Mocha (or Moka) can mean many things: 1) a chocolate-and-coffee beverage; 2) a port city in Yemen that is a famous coffee marketplace; 3) a variety of coffee bean; and 4) a stovetop espresso pot first produced by Bialetti Industries in 1933. This coffee and chocolate liqueur (spelled MOCA for distinction) could have been inspired by any of the above, and if you choose to use authentic Yemeni Mocha coffee beans, you will support that point.

Similar to the kinship of coffee and toasted nuts, coffee and chocolate share many flavor characteristics, including a balance of acidity and bitterness, toasted flavors from roasting, and an affinity for sweetening, all of which make them especially easy to like in liqueur.

MAKES ABOUT 1 QUART

1½ cups vodka (80–100 proof)

1½ cups brandy (80 proof)

1 cup (4 ounces) cacao nibs

1 cup (4 ounces) medium-roast coffee beans, cracked

1¼ cups Brown Simple Syrup (page 24)

1. Combine the vodka, brandy, cacao nibs, and coffee beans in a half-gallon jar. Stir to moisten everything.

2. Seal the jar and put it in a cool, dark cabinet until the liquid smells and tastes strongly of chocolate and coffee, 3 to 5 days.

3. Strain the mixture with a mesh strainer into a clean quart jar. Do not push on the solids to extract more liquid.

4. Stir in the simple syrup.

5. Seal and store in the refrigerator. Use within 6 months.

Y *Santé!* *Shake with ice — instant Mocha Martini!*

Green Honey

Matcha, finely milled high-quality green tea powder, is the center-piece of the Japanese tea ceremony. The method for powdering steamed dried tea leaves was developed in Song Dynasty China (960 to 1279). The practice of whipping matcha in hot water became popular, and consumption of such tea was codified into ritual by Zen Buddhists.

In modern times, matcha has become popular as a flavoring/coloring agent for mochi and soba noodles, green tea ice cream, and candies. It is prized for its antioxidant prowess. And what a color! Green Honey liqueur is vibrant apple green, with a light grassy perfume.

MAKES ABOUT 1 QUART

1 fifth (750 ml/3¼ cups) vodka
   (80–100 proof)
8 green tea bags
¼ cup matcha powder
   Grated zest of 3 limes
¾ cup mild honey, like clover
   or orange blossom

1. Combine the vodka, tea bags, matcha, lime zest, and honey in a half-gallon jar. Stir to moisten everything.

2. Seal the jar and put it in a cool, dark cabinet until the liquid smells and tastes strongly of green tea, 3 to 5 days.

3. Strain the mixture with a fine-mesh strainer. Do not push on the solids to extract more liquid.

4. Seal and store in a cool, dark cabinet. Use within 1 year.

Y *Cheers!* *Refreshing over ice, garnished with a wedge of lime, and soothing served warm, as you would sake.*

Chai-namon

You could blend together a cabinetful of spices to flavor this exotic liqueur, or you could just crack open a box of chai tea bags, break apart a few cinnamon sticks, and call it a day. Chai tea, the easy-to-love spiced black tea, is an effortless way to obtain huge flavor impact with minimum effort. Because alcohol is super-adept at hooking up with flavor compounds, steeping the tea bags in hot water to release their flavor is unnecessary. Just mix everything together and let it do its thing. But take a few deep breaths before you close the jar — this one smells as good as it tastes.

MAKES ABOUT 1 QUART

1½ cups vodka (80–100 proof)
1½ cups brandy (80 proof)
 4 chai tea bags
 4 cinnamon sticks, cracked
 1 cup Brown Simple Syrup (page 24)

1. Combine the vodka, brandy, chai tea bags, and cinnamon sticks in a half-gallon jar. Stir to moisten everything.

2. Seal the jar and put it in a cool, dark cabinet until the liquid smells and tastes strongly of spices, 3 to 5 days.

3. Strain the mixture with a mesh strainer into a clean quart jar. Do not push on the solids to extract more liquid.

4. Stir in the simple syrup.

5. Seal and store in the refrigerator. Use within 1 year.

Y *Salut!* *Use it to spike warm cider or make a Spiced Red Wine (page 253).*

White Fig

White tea possesses a fragile floral fragrance that is enhanced here by the essence of pale Turkish figs. It is a delicate combination that would be lost as a tea but is fine-tuned when captured in alcohol. I use dry gin, which is less aromatic than Dutch gin, to eliminate extraneous flavor elements.

MAKES ABOUT 1 QUART

1   fifth (750 ml/3¼ cups) English-style gin (86 proof)

1½ cups (3 ounces) loose white tea leaves

12   dried Turkish (or any pale-colored) figs, chopped

1¼ cups Simple Syrup (page 24)

1. Combine the gin, white tea, and figs in a half-gallon jar. Stir to moisten everything.

2. Seal the jar and put it in a cool, dark cabinet until the liquid smells and tastes subtly of tea and fruit, about 5 days.

3. Strain the mixture with a mesh strainer into a clean quart jar. Do not push on the solids to extract more liquid.

4. Stir in the simple syrup.

5. Seal and store in a cool, dark cabinet. Use within 1 year.

Y *Skål!* *A beautiful liqueur for perfuming a gin Martini or an icy glass of lemonade.*

Smokin'

Lapsang Souchong tea leaves are fermented into black tea and then dried over smoky pine fires, lending this highly aromatic tea a resinous flavor. In this fire-engine red liqueur, that smoky base is underscored with additions of pimentón (Spanish smoked paprika) and a spike of smoked black pepper. The overall effect is a knockout; use it to smoke up a Manhattan.

MAKES ABOUT 1 QUART

1¼ cups vodka (80–100 proof)

1¼ cups peaty (smoky) Islay single-malt Scotch, like Laphroaig

4 Lapsang Souchong tea bags

2 tablespoons smoked paprika (pimentón)

1 teaspoon smoked black pepper

1½ cups Brown Simple Syrup (page 24)

1. Combine the vodka, Scotch, tea bags, paprika, and black pepper in a half-gallon jar. Stir to moisten everything.

2. Seal the jar and put it in a cool, dark cabinet until the liquid smells and tastes strongly of smoke, 3 to 5 days.

3. Strain the mixture with a fine mesh strainer. Do not push on the solids to extract more liquid.

4. Stir in the simple syrup.

5. Seal and store in a cool, dark cabinet. Use within 1 year.

Y *L'chaim!* *Liven things up with a Smokin' Mary (page 242) or a Volcano (page 248).*

Tannin Teaser

Tannins are components in some plants that bind to and precipitate proteins and alkaloids, acting as a deterrent to predators and as an insecticide. When you drink tea, red wine, or some fruit juices (grape or apple in particular), tannins in those products create a drying, puckering sensation in the mouth. In excess, this reaction can be unpleasant, but when controlled, the drying effect is translated by our brains as thirst, making the liquid in the tea, juice, or wine feel more refreshing.

The tannins in Tannin Teaser come from black tea leaves and persimmons. Unripe persimmon, particularly the Hachiya variety (which is heart-shaped), is especially high in tannins.

MAKES ABOUT 1 QUART

1 fifth (750 ml/3¼ cups) vodka (80-100 proof)
6 Chinese black tea bags
2 unripe Hachiya persimmons
½ cup (2 ounces) cacao nibs
1 cup brewed black tea
1 cup palm sugar

1. Combine the vodka, tea bags, persimmons, and cacao nibs in a half-gallon jar. Stir to moisten everything.

2. Seal the jar and put it in a cool, dark cabinet until a taste instantly puckers the tongue, 3 to 5 days.

3. While the liqueur is maturing, make tea-flavored syrup by combining the brewed black tea and palm sugar in a small saucepan. Heat over medium heat until the mixture turns translucent and bubbles form around the edge. Do not allow the mixture to boil.

4. Strain the mixture with a mesh strainer into a clean quart jar. Do not push on the solids to extract more liquid.

5. Stir in the tea syrup.

6. Seal and store in a cool, dark cabinet. Use within 1 year.

....

Y *Santé! Makes for a sultry Gin and Tonic or Screwdriver.*

Moroccan Mint

Maghreb-style mint tea (green tea with mint leaves) is a drink of hospitality throughout North Africa, served whenever there are guests. It is always sweetened. Like matcha in Japan, the serving of Maghreb tea is highly ritualized in Morocco, with the head of the house pouring tea from a long spouted pot held at an impressive height above the guest's glass. The cascade of tea hitting its mark with nary a drop spilled is equivalent to a perfectly executed high dive. The virtuosity and refreshing comfort of Moroccan mint tea is captured beautifully in this delicate liqueur.

MAKES ABOUT 1 QUART

1 **fifth (750 ml/3¼ cups) vodka (80-100 proof)**

6 **green tea bags**

2 **cups dried mint**

¼ **cup honey**

¾ **cup Simple Syrup (page 24)**

1. Combine the vodka, tea bags, mint, and honey in a half-gallon jar. Stir to moisten everything.

2. Seal the jar and put it in a cool, dark cabinet until the liquid smells and tastes strongly of mint, 3 to 5 days.

3. Strain the mixture with a mesh strainer into a clean quart jar. Do not push on the solids to extract more liquid.

4. Stir in the simple syrup.

5. Seal and store in a cool, dark cabinet. Use within 1 year.

Y *Bottoms Up!* *Splash over ice and add a wedge of lime when heat and humidity overwhelm.*

Chocolate Night

It was a dark and sultry night, heady with the scent of espresso, cocoa, and barely burnt sugar — a night to be savored sip by bitter-sweet sip. This slightly opaque, naturally thick liqueur is loaded with microscopic flavor-bursting particles. If you prefer a transparent liqueur, you can strain the tincture through several layers of damp cheesecloth set in the strainer, but I advise against it. The flavor is so much fuller if you don't, and the only downside is having to shake the bottle each time you pour yourself yet another decadent drink.

MAKES ABOUT 1 QUART

- 1 tablespoon unsweetened cocoa powder
- 1¼ cups (5 ounces) cacao nibs
- ⅓ cup brewed espresso
- 2 cups vodka (80–100 proof)
- 1 cup brandy (80 proof)
- 1 cup Simple Syrup (page 24)
- ¼ cup Caramelized Simple Syrup (page 24)

1. Mix the cocoa powder, cacao nibs, and espresso in a bowl to moisten.

2. Combine the cocoa mixture, vodka, and brandy in a half-gallon jar.

3. Seal the jar and shake vigorously. Put it in a cool, dark cabinet until the liquid tastes strongly of chocolate, 2 to 3 days, shaking well every day.

4. Strain the mixture with a fine-mesh strainer into a clean quart jar. Do not push on the solids to extract more liquid.

5. Stir in both simple syrups.

6. Seal and store in a cool, dark cabinet. Use within 1 year.

🍸 *Prost!* *Makes a delicious Mocha Manhattan with a few drops of chocolate bitters.*

Coco-Loco

Copycat Crème de Cacao

As unadorned and sublime as a Hershey bar, this transparent, barely tinted liqueur is the disembodied spirit of roasted cocoa. The alcohol absorbs all of the nuanced chocolate flavor from cacao nibs (cracked roasted cocoa beans). Amended with the fragrance of real vanilla and sugared to bittersweetness, this is an all-purpose chocolate liqueur, great in Chocolate Martinis.

MAKES ABOUT 1 QUART

1 fifth (750 ml/3¼ cups) vodka (80–100 proof)
1½ cups (6 ounces) cacao nibs
1 vanilla bean (Madagascar or Bourbon), split
1¼ cups Simple Syrup (page 24)

1. Combine the vodka, cacao nibs, and vanilla in a half-gallon jar. Stir to moisten everything.

2. Seal the jar and put it in a cool, dark cabinet until the liquid tastes strongly of chocolate, 3 to 5 days.

3. Strain the mixture with a mesh strainer lined with several layers of dampened cheesecloth into a clean quart jar. Do not push on the solids to extract more liquid.

4. Stir in the simple syrup.

5. Seal and store in a cool, dark cabinet. Use within 1 year.

Y *Salut!* Lots of options: Banshee (page 239), Brandy Al (page 239), Chocolate Xander (page 240), or Mocha Nut, pictured here (page 240).

Sweet Chocolate

The snobbery surrounding premium, gourmet chocolate made with high percentages of cocoa bean (70, 80, even 100 percent) has led to the brainless perception that everything in a chocolate bar's ingredient list other than the beans (sugar, cream, vanilla, or butter) is an unwelcome adulterant. There is a certain fascist logic to striving for 100-percent purity, but by avoiding the beautiful offspring born from disparate elements, you never learn that a little sugar boldly brings the fruitiness forward, and that a touch of dairy relaxes the brittle snap of dark chocolate, softening its militaristic salute into an affable handshake. This liqueur is friendly; you'll want to take it out for a drink.

MAKES ABOUT 1 QUART

½ cup sweetened condensed milk
¼ cup unsweetened cocoa powder
1 cup (4 ounces) cacao nibs
2 cups vodka (80–100 proof)
1 cup brandy (80 proof)
1 cup Caramelized Simple
    Syrup (page 24)

1. With a small whisk in a small saucepan, mix the condensed milk and cocoa powder into a smooth paste. Bring to a simmer over medium-low heat, stirring constantly. Let cool.

2. Combine the cocoa mixture, cacao nibs, vodka, and brandy in a half-gallon jar.

3. Seal the jar and shake vigorously. Put it in a cool, dark cabinet until the liquid tastes strongly of chocolate, 3 to 5 days, shaking well every day.

4. Strain the mixture with a fine-mesh strainer lined with several layers of damp cheesecloth into a clean quart jar. Do not push on the solids to extract more liquid.

5. Stir in the simple syrup.

6. Seal and store in a cool, dark cabinet. Use within 1 year.

Y **Skål!** *Pour over a scoop of vanilla and a scoop of coffee ice cream for a just dessert.*

Chocolate Orange Peel

When I was eight years old, I was a connoisseur of mass-market chocolate. I mastered an appreciation for all four fillings of a Sky Bar, but I was certain I would never be mature enough to savor the adults-only bitterness of chocolate-covered orange peel. Boy, was I wrong.

Bitter orange (a.k.a. Seville orange) is grown for its peel, which is thick and saturated with orange oil. The same oil is in the zest of conventional oranges, but it is not as rich and it lacks that defining bitterness. To get the right flavor for this liqueur, include a little bit of the white pith beneath the skin when you grate the zest. The bitter alkaloids in the zest will be absorbed into the alcohol, yielding a perfect blend for bittersweet orange elixir. Maturity has its perks.

MAKES ABOUT 1 QUART

2 tablespoons unsweetened cocoa powder

⅓ cup fresh orange juice

1 cup (4 ounces) cacao nibs

2 cups vodka (80–100 proof)

1 cup brandy (80 proof)

Finely grated zest (plus some of the white pith beneath the zest) of 4 oranges

1 cup Simple Syrup (page 24)

1. Mix the cocoa powder and orange juice into a smooth paste using small whisk in a small bowl.

2. Combine the cocoa mixture, cacao nibs, vodka, brandy, and orange zest in a half-gallon jar.

3. Seal the jar and shake vigorously. Put it in a cool, dark cabinet until the liquid smells of orange and tastes of chocolate, 3 to 5 days, shaking well every day. The longer tincturing time increases the bitterness from the orange peel, which some people prefer.

4. Strain the mixture with a fine-mesh strainer. Do not push on the solids to extract more liquid.

5. Stir in the simple syrup.

6. Seal and store in a cool, dark cabinet. Use within 1 year.

Y *Sláinte!* *Spike a glass of iced coffee.*

CREAMY LIQUEURS

CREAM ALWAYS RISES TO THE TOP, AND THERE'S NO EXCEPTION IN THE WORLD OF LIQUEURS. Creamy liqueurs are considered the richest, most elegant, and most desirable of potables. Few single ingredients change the nature of liqueurs so dramatically as cream. A shift in the type of sugar can alter color and flavor slightly; a different alcohol base has similar effect; but adding cream makes the whole system switch gears. The beverage moves from fluid toward solid, and its essence, once merely fruity or herbal or sweet, all at once becomes both more substantial and more decadent.

The process of making cream liqueurs has a few twists on the standard process. For one thing, creamy liqueurs use a dairy-based simple syrup that is slightly more complicated to assemble and has to be kept refrigerated.

I use three different creamy sweeteners for different styles of creamy liqueurs: Creamy Simple Syrup (page 25) as an all-purpose sweetener, Brown Cow Simple Syrup (page 25) for whiskey and brandy cream liqueurs, and Tangy-Creamy Simple Syrup (page 25) for fresh-fruit cream liqueurs. They all use sweetened condensed milk as a main ingredient.

Milk is an emulsion in which protein and fat are suspended in water. It's inherently unstable, and when making liqueur, a stable and viscous dairy product is vital for long-term storage. Sweetened condensed milk is made by mixing whole milk with sugar (roughly two parts milk to one part sugar) and cooking off about 60 percent of the water

to create a thick, very sweet liquid. It was developed in the mid-nineteenth century as a means of preserving milk, which before then was only available raw and was highly perishable. Condensing milk naturally pasteurizes it, and the sterile canning process means it can be stored for months without refrigeration.

Even with the advantages of condensed milk, adding protein to a liqueur makes it more perishable. Unlike most liqueurs, cream liqueurs need to be refrigerated immediately after the dairy is added, and even then they have a shelf life of about a month, as opposed to almost a year.

As they sit, homemade cream liqueurs are apt to separate. Commercial cream liqueurs are mechanically emulsified and hence less prone to separating, but home cooks do not have the right equipment, so some separation is inevitable. The liqueurs are easily blended with a brisk shake before serving.

Irish Cream

Copycat Baileys Irish Cream

The most famous cream liqueur is a newborn in the world of cordials. A mixture of Irish whiskey and cream, it was launched in 1974 by Gilbey's (of gin fame). The Bailey name, with the accompanying R.A. Bailey signature on the foil cap, is fictional. Baileys Irish Cream quickly became internationally popular and spawned dozens of whiskey-and-cream imitators. It is most famously imbibed in a version of Irish Coffee.

MAKES ABOUT 1 QUART

2 cups Irish whiskey (80 proof)

1½ cups Brown Cow Simple Syrup (page 25)

1. Combine the whiskey and simple syrup in a half-gallon jar.

2. Seal the jar and store in the refrigerator until the flavors taste blended, 1 to 2 days. Keep refrigerated and use within 1 month.

NOTE: After 2 weeks in the refrigerator, the cream from the simple syrup may rise to the top of the liqueur. If this happens, shake the mixture to redistribute the cream.

Y *Cheers!* *Delicious sipped straight up, and heavenly in a B-52 (page 239) or Creamy Irish Coffee (page 240).*

White Russian

Named for the classic cocktail made with vodka, coffee liqueur, and cream, White Russian liqueur is a grab-and-go cocktail in a bottle. Lighter-roast coffee has more aroma and natural acidity than dark-roast beans, which tend to be bitter, so I prefer it for most coffee liqueurs. The brown sugar syrup reinforces the roasted notes in the coffee. Use it to simultaneously spike and soothe a cup of black coffee.

MAKES ABOUT 1 QUART

3 cups vodka (80–100 proof)

1½ cups (7½ ounces) medium-roast coffee beans, coarsely cracked

½ cup Brown Cow Simple Syrup (page 25)

1. Combine the vodka and coffee beans in a half-gallon jar.

2. Seal the jar and store in a cool, dark cabinet until the liquid tastes and smells strongly of coffee, 3 to 5 days.

3. Strain the mixture with a mesh strainer into a clean quart jar.

4. Stir in the simple syrup.

5. Seal the jar and store in the refrigerator until the flavors taste blended, about 2 days. Keep refrigerated and use within 1 month.

NOTE: After 2 weeks in the refrigerator, the cream from the simple syrup may rise to the top of the liqueur. If this happens, shake the mixture to redistribute the cream.

Y *L'chaim!* *The obvious choice for making a Streamlined White Russian (page 240).*

Eggnog

Eggnog, the wassailing mixture of frothed egg, sugar, cream, and booze, is an essential part of Anglo holiday feasting. The name was derived either from Middle English noggin, a small wooden mug for serving alcohol, or condensed from the words egg and grog (a Colonial term for a drink containing rum). Either way, the drink is decidedly British, crossing the Atlantic early on in the birth of the Colonies. An island version, Coquito, uses coconut milk for the cream, and rum instead of brandy.

MAKES ABOUT 1 QUART

½ cup Creamy Simple Syrup (page 25)
2 egg yolks
1 teaspoon pure vanilla extract
   Pinch of ground nutmeg
2 cups brandy (80 proof)

1. Heat the simple syrup in a small saucepan over medium heat until bubbling, stirring frequently.

2. Mix the egg yolks, vanilla, and nutmeg in a small bowl. Add the warm simple syrup into the egg yolk mixture a spoonful at a time. Once half of the syrup has been incorporated in this way, add the rest in a slow stream.

3. Combine the brandy and egg yolk mixture in a half-gallon jar.

4. Seal the jar and store in the refrigerator until the flavors taste blended, 1 to 2 days. Keep refrigerated and use within 1 month.

NOTE: After 2 weeks in the refrigerator, the cream from the simple syrup may rise to the top of the liqueur. If this happens, shake the mixture to redistribute the cream.

Y *Santé!* *A Brandy Coquito (page 240) or Oaxaca Eggnog (page 240) will warm your heart.*

Vanilla Cream

This not-so-plain vanilla of cream liqueurs has all the delicate floral and fruity nuance of vanilla bean, and since there is little else to modify its purity, it encompasses the versatility of vanilla as well. It is an all-purpose creamy concoction for making adults-only milk shakes and floats, experimenting with creamy Martinis, or spiking a cup of hot coffee, chai tea, or cocoa.

MAKES ABOUT 1 QUART

2 cups vodka (80 proof)
3 vanilla beans (Madagascar or Bourbon), split
½ of a whole nutmeg
1½ cups Creamy Simple Syrup (page 25)

1. Combine the vodka, vanilla, and nutmeg in a half-gallon jar.

2. Seal the jar and store in a cool, dark cabinet until fragrant, about 3 days.

3. Remove the vanilla beans and nutmeg.

4. Stir in the simple syrup.

5. Seal and store in the refrigerator until the flavors taste blended, 1 to 2 days. Keep refrigerated and use within 1 month.

NOTE: After 2 weeks in the refrigerator, the cream from the simple syrup may rise to the top of the liqueur. If this happens, shake the mixture to redistribute the cream.

Strawberry Yogurt

Knock back a glass of this fresher-than-fresh, boozy strawberry smoothie and transport your taste buds back in time. The alcohol locks onto and preserves the ripe berry flavor, allowing you to mix up a batch at the height of strawberry season and savor its essence weeks later. With the flavor of a bowl of strawberry ice cream and the potency of a shot of ice-cold vodka, this pale pink liqueur vibrates deliciously between innocence and corruption.

MAKES ABOUT 1 QUART

2 cups vodka (80 proof)
1 pint fresh strawberries, trimmed and finely chopped, or 12 oz frozen strawberries
1 vanilla bean (Madagascar or Bourbon), split
1½ cups Tangy-Creamy Simple Syrup (page 25)

1. Combine the vodka, strawberries, and vanilla in a half-gallon jar.

2. Seal the jar and store in a cool, dark cabinet until fragrant, about 5 days.

3. Strain the mixture with a fine-mesh strainer into a clean quart jar.

4. Stir in the simple syrup.

5. Seal and store in the refrigerator until the flavors taste blended, 1 to 2 days. Keep refrigerated and use within 1 month.

NOTE: After 2 weeks in the refrigerator, the cream from the simple syrup may rise to the top of the liqueur. If this happens, shake the mixture to redistribute the cream.

🍸 *Salut!* *Serve chilled in a rocks glass over ice with shortbread cookies for dipping.*

Orange Dreamsicle

Lounging by the community swimming hole, listening for the ice cream truck, then seeing my sister's sweaty brown face smudged with sticky swipes of orange sherbet — all those steamy suburban evenings swirl into one satisfying slurp of summer whenever I chug down a tumbler of this fragrant, fruity, creamy liqueur. Unapologetically inspired by orange Creamsicles (I know there are other Popsicle flavors, but do they really count?), this simple, dairy-rich, sweet citrus concoction is a time traveler, simultaneously satisfying the most discerning contemporary tastes and the most nostalgic longings for childhood.

MAKES ABOUT 1 QUART

2 cups vodka (80 proof)
Finely grated zest of 3 oranges
1½ cups Creamy Simple Syrup (page 25)

1. Combine the vodka and orange zest in a half-gallon jar. Seal the jar and store in a cool, dark cabinet until fragrant, about 5 days.

2. Strain the mixture with a fine-mesh strainer into a clean quart jar.

3. Stir in the simple syrup.

4. Seal and store in the refrigerator until the flavors taste blended, 1 to 2 days. Keep refrigerated and use within 1 month.

NOTE: After 2 weeks in the refrigerator, the cream from the simple syrup may rise to the top of the liqueur. If this happens, shake the mixture to redistribute the cream.

Y *Prost!* *Serve icy cold on a summer night.*

Apple Sour Cream

Decades ago, when I was a chef in a small boutique restaurant in Philadelphia, our most popular dessert was a deep-dish apple–sour cream pie with a walnut streusel topping. This liqueur is the liquid incarnation of that sublime creation. Tangy and rich, mildly fruity, and zanily nutty — its pleasures just don't stop. Everyone I have offered a sip to ends up polishing off the whole bottle.

MAKES ABOUT 1 QUART

2 cups vodka (80 proof)
3 large apples, seeded and finely chopped
4 ounces walnut pieces, toasted and ground
2 cinnamon sticks, cracked
1½ cups Tangy-Creamy Simple Syrup (page 25)

1. Combine the vodka, apples, walnuts, and cinnamon in a half-gallon jar. Seal the jar and store in a cool, dark cabinet until fragrant, about 5 days.

2. Strain the mixture with a fine-mesh strainer into a clean quart jar.

3. Stir in the simple syrup.

4. Seal and store in the refrigerator until the flavors taste blended, 1 to 2 days. Keep refrigerated and use within 1 month.

NOTE: After 2 weeks in the refrigerator, the cream from the simple syrup may rise to the top of the liqueur. If this happens, shake the mixture to redistribute the cream.

Y *Sláinte!* *Makes a belly-busting creamy Appletini.*

Praline Peach

Peaches and almond praline are intimately united in my taste buds of memory. It could be because I associate both of them with a summer spent in an organic garden in Louisville, Kentucky, or because they are a natural flavor pairing (the kernel of a peach pit is a form of bitter almond). I have made this liqueur with both white sugar and brown sugar syrups. The color is purer with white (a glorious pastel peachy orange), but the praline flavor is way better with brown. Since my passion for eating and drinking has always been centered more in my mouth than my eyes, I use the brown syrup every time.

MAKES ABOUT 1 QUART

2 cups vodka (80 proof)

3 yellow peaches, pitted
   and finely chopped

1 vanilla bean (Madagascar or
   Bourbon), split

1½ cups Brown Cow Simple Syrup
   (page 25)

1 teaspoon pure almond extract

1. Combine the vodka, peaches, and vanilla in a half-gallon jar. Seal the jar and store in a cool, dark cabinet until fragrant, about 5 days.

2. Strain the mixture with a fine-mesh strainer into a clean quart jar.

3. Stir in the simple syrup and extract.

4. Seal and store in the refrigerator until the flavors taste blended, 1 to 2 days. Keep refrigerated and use within 1 month.

NOTE: After 2 weeks in the refrigerator, the cream from the simple syrup may rise to the top of the liqueur. If this happens, shake the mixture to redistribute the cream.

Y *Skål!* *Sip warm, spiked with a thimble of bourbon or brandy.*

Caramel Crème

Copycat Dulce de Leche

M-m-m-milk jam! Dulce de leche, the Spanish cooked sweet-milk pre-serve, is commonly spread on bread for breakfast or snacks or turned into a dessert sauce. Recently it has become the base for a number of boutique liqueurs. Use this lovely liqueur in a Caramel Martini or in place of crème de cacao for a caramelized Brandy Alexander.

MAKES ABOUT 1 QUART

2¼ cups dark rum (80 proof)
½ vanilla bean (Madagascar or Bourbon), split
1 (14-ounce) can sweetened condensed milk
Pinch of fine sea salt

1. Combine the rum and vanilla in a half-gallon jar. Seal the jar and store in a cool, dark cabinet until fragrant, about 3 days.

2. **TO MAKE THE DULCE DE LECHE:** Preheat the oven to 425°F. Pour the condensed milk into a glass pie plate or shallow glass baking dish and stir in the salt. Cover it tightly with aluminum foil. Set the pie plate in a roasting pan and add hot water to the roasting pan until the water comes halfway up the sides of the pie plate. Make sure the edges of the foil are not hanging in the water.

Bake until deeply browned, about 1 hour, adding more water if the level in the roasting pan gets low. Remove from the oven and let cool; whisk the dulce de leche until smooth. (You can make this ahead and store in the refrigerator for up to 1 month; warm gently in a warm water bath before using.)

3. Remove the vanilla bean from the rum. Add the dulce de leche.

4. Seal the jar, and shake to combine. Store in the refrigerator until the flavors taste blended, about 1 day. Keep refrigerated and use within 1 month.

NOTE: After 2 weeks in the refrigerator, the cream from the simple syrup may rise to the top of the liqueur. If this happens, shake the mixture to redistribute the cream.

Banana Split

In 2004 the city of Latrobe, Pennsylvania, was certified as the official birthplace of the banana split, 100 years after its creation. First made by soda jerk David Strickler at the Tassel Pharmacy, the banana split, bursting with a variety of flavors, was a staple of soda fountains for most of the twentieth century, vying with the simpler and arguably more elegant hot fudge sundae for a spot as the most iconic ice cream treat of all time. This liqueur captures three of the split's essential components — bananas, chocolate syrup, and vanilla ice cream — in a creamy confection.

MAKES ABOUT 1 QUART

2 cups light rum (80 proof)
3 bananas, peeled and finely chopped
1 cup (4 ounces) cacao nibs
1 vanilla bean (Madagascar
   or Bourbon), split
1½ cups Creamy Simple Syrup (page 25)

1. Combine the rum, bananas, cacao nibs, and vanilla in a half-gallon jar. Seal the jar and store in a cool, dark cabinet until fragrant, about 5 days.

2. Strain the mixture with a fine-mesh strainer into a clean quart jar.

3. Stir in the simple syrup.

4. Seal and store in the refrigerator until the flavors taste blended, 1 to 2 days. Keep refrigerated and use within 1 month.

NOTE: After 2 weeks in the refrigerator, the cream from the simple syrup may rise to the top of the liqueur. If this happens, shake the mixture to redistribute the cream.

Y *Bottoms Up!* Blend with ice for an instant Banana Daiquiri.

Lemon Mousse

Lemon and cream generally don't play nicely together — the one being highly acidic and the other prone to curdling. Most recipes keep the two quarantined, but here, using lemon zest instead of lemon juice eliminates the acids. All that's left is a ton of fragrant lemon-scented oil that marries beautifully with a simple syrup to create a deliciously curious couple. Lemon Mousse is a lovely pastel yellow, but its brilliant lemon flavor is anything but muted.

MAKES ABOUT 1 QUART

2 cups vodka (80 proof)

Finely grated zest of 4 lemons

1½ cups Creamy Simple Syrup (page 25)

1. Combine the vodka and lemon zest in a half-gallon jar. Seal the jar and store in a cool, dark cabinet until fragrant, about 5 days.

2. Strain out the mixture with a fine-mesh strainer into a clean quart jar.

3. Stir in the simple syrup.

4. Seal and store in the refrigerator until the flavors taste blended, 1 to 2 days. Keep refrigerated and use within 1 month.

NOTE: After 2 weeks in the refrigerator, the cream from the simple syrup may rise to the top of the liqueur. If this happens, shake the mixture to redistribute the cream.

Y **Prost!** *Spoon over berries or sip in a Lemon Cooler (1 part Lemon Mousse and 2 parts lemon-lime soda).*

Chocolate Milk

Copycat Vermeer Dutch Chocolate Cream

My cooking career commenced with chocolate milk. I made it every day after school, and my technique, though self-taught, was flawless. Chocolate syrup (I was a devotee of Bosco) was drizzled in the glass first, followed by just enough milk to match its volume, tablespoon for tablespoon. The syrup had to be completely dissolved in the first round. Add too much milk too soon and inerasable chocolate skids irreparably marred the glass. If I did my job well, the rest was a breeze — just thin the chocolate base with more milk and drink up.

This recipe is nearly as straightforward. The biggest difference is that you have to make your own chocolate syrup; commercial brands are too sweet for this adults-only chocolate milk.

MAKES ABOUT 1 QUART

¾ cup unsweetened cocoa powder
⅔ cup sugar
    Pinch of fine sea salt
1 cup water
2 cups vodka (80 proof)
1 cup Creamy Simple Syrup (page 25)

1. Combine the cocoa powder, sugar, and salt in a saucepan. Slowly whisk in the water until smooth. Turn the heat to low and bring to a simmer, stirring often. Simmer for 2 minutes, stirring frequently. Let cool.

2. Combine the vodka, chocolate syrup, and simple syrup in a half-gallon jar.

3. Seal the jar and store in the refrigerator until the flavors taste blended, 1 to 2 days. Keep refrigerated and use within 1 month.

NOTE: After 2 weeks in the refrigerator, the cream from the simple syrup may rise to the top of the liqueur. If this happens, shake the mixture to redistribute the cream.

Y *Sláinte!* Gulp a glass well-chilled, with a cookie chaser.

CARAMEL, SYRUP & BUTTERSCOTCH LIQUEURS

ALL SUGAR IS SWEET, BUT NO SUGAR IS JUST SWEET; they vary considerably by their degree of processing. Raw sugars are minimally processed, and white sugars and brown sugars are fully processed. (See page 20 for more about sugars.) Almost all of the previous recipes in these pages are made with fully processed sugars.

In this chapter, we are working with unrefined and caramelized sugars. They all have subtle aromatics, varying consistencies, and shifting hues — enough nuance to make them interesting flavoring agents in their own right.

One of the first things to happen in any sugar-refining process is that the stock (usually sugarcane or beets) is milled to extract its juices. The juices are boiled until the solid sweet particles concentrate to about 60 percent by weight. Another 10 percent of water is taken out by centrifuging, resulting in a dark brown paste that is supersaturated with sugar crystals. At this point the sugar can be sold as Japanese black sugar or soft jaggery.

The supersaturated sugar syrup is then seeded with sugar crystals, causing a chain reaction that precipitates a mass of coarse-grained, golden-hued sugar crystals coated with molasses. At this stage, the sugar can be left as damp crystals (called muscovado or Barbados sugar) or dried and formed into cakes (solid jaggery). Further refining of the damp sugar crystals by centrifuge draws off the molasses coating, leaving behind relatively dry golden-hued sugar crystals that are sold as demerara or turbinado sugar. When all of the molasses has been cast off, the resulting granulated sugar is pure white.

Completely processed sugar can be flavored after processing. Brown sugar is white sugar that is mixed with molasses. The more molasses, the darker the brown sugar.

Caramel is white sugar that has been heated. When sugar is heated enough to melt, it doesn't just change color — it also changes structure. From the colorless and odorless sweet crystals emerge hundreds of new compounds, some sour, some bitter, and some aromatic. The hotter the sugar gets, the less like granulated sugar it becomes, eventually turning dark, molten, and bitter. Butterscotch is caramel with milk solids added to make a creamy confection.

The following recipes use these types of sugars to create subtly aromatic, golden-hued liqueurs that are much more than just sweet.

Caramel Cordial

The combination of caramelized sugar syrup and vanilla bean yields a liquid form of chewy vanilla caramels. Take candy into a sophisticated realm by making a Salted Caramel Martini (shown at right) with three parts vodka, one part Caramel Cordial, and a pinch of fine sea salt. I like using Halen Môn Gold, a flaked salt from Wales that is smoked over oak — delicious!

MAKES ABOUT 1 QUART

1 cup vodka (80–100 proof)
1 cup brandy (80 proof)
2 vanilla beans (Madagascar or Bourbon), split
1¼ cups Caramelized Simple Syrup (page 24)

1. Combine the vodka, brandy, vanilla, and simple syrup in a quart jar. Stir to moisten everything.

2. Seal the jar and put it in a cool, dark cabinet until the liquid smells and tastes strongly of vanilla caramel, about 2 days.

3. Strain the mixture with a mesh strainer into a clean quart jar. Do not push on the solids to extract more liquid.

4. Seal and store in a cool, dark cabinet. Use within 1 year.

Y **Cheers!** *Kick up your heels with a Caramel Mule (page 255).*

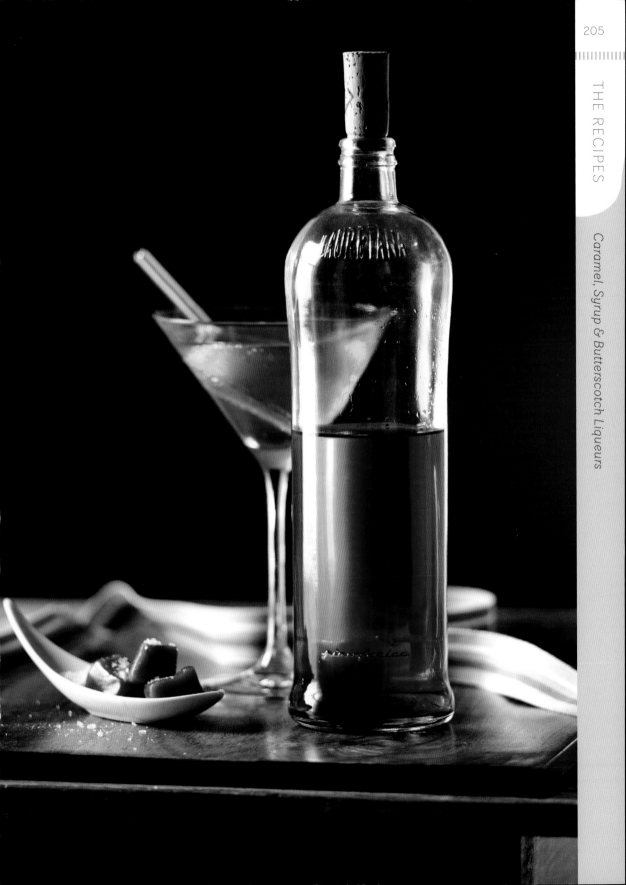

Caramel Apple

The essence of apple is captured in bourbon and infused with cara-melized sugar to create the embodied spirit of a caramel apple. Pair it with apple-flavored vodka for a Caramel Appletini (page 247), or spike a cup of warm spiced apple cider for a wintery nightcap.

MAKES ABOUT 1 QUART

3 sweet apples, like Honeycrisp, Golden Delicious, or Winesap, stemmed and coarsely shredded

1½ cups Caramelized Simple Syrup (page 24)

2 cups bourbon (80 proof)

2 cinnamon sticks, cracked

1. Muddle the shredded apples and simple syrup with a wooden spoon in a half-gallon jar. Add the bourbon and cinnamon sticks. Stir to moisten everything.

2. Seal the jar and put it in a cool, dark cabinet until the liquid smells and tastes strongly of apple, about 5 days.

3. Strain the mixture with a mesh strainer into a clean quart jar. Do not push on the solids to extract more liquid.

4. Seal and store in a cool, dark cabinet. Use within 1 year.

Butter-Scotch

Real butterscotch, a caramel candy made with brown sugar and butter, doesn't contain any real Scotch. What a rip-off! This recipe is designed to right that wrong. Blended Scotch is combined with milk solids (skimmed from melted butter) and caramel. The liqueur has all of the mind-numbing sugar rush of butterscotch candy upended by the mind-numbing alcohol rush of 10-year-old Highland Scotch.

MAKES ABOUT 1 QUART

4 ounces (1 stick) unsalted butter, cut into small pieces

1½ cups Caramelized Simple Syrup (page 24)

1¾ cups blended Scotch or single malt Highland Scotch (86 proof)

1 vanilla bean (Madagascar or Bourbon), split

1. Melt the butter over medium heat in a small saucepan. As foam rises to the surface, skim and reserve. Continue heating until the melted butter looks clear and there are pale solids collected on the bottom of the pot. The butter is now clarified. Skim off the clear liquid (you will have about 6 tablespoons) and reserve to use as clarified butter in other recipes. It will stay fresh in the refrigerator in a tightly closed container for 6 months.

2. Add the reserved foam to the pale milky solids in the bottom of the pan. Add the simple syrup and stir to combine. If necessary, you can heat the mixture briefly to help it come together.

3. Combine the butter-syrup mixture, Scotch, and vanilla in a 1-quart jar.

4. Seal the jar and put it in a cool, dark cabinet until the liquid smells and tastes strongly of vanilla caramel, about 2 days.

5. Put the mixture in the freezer for about 30 minutes. Any fat remaining from the butter will become solid.

6. Strain the mixture with a mesh strainer into a clean quart jar. Do not push on the solids to extract more liquid.

7. Seal and store in a cool, dark cabinet. Use within 1 year.

Y *Skål!* *A natural flavor enhancer for a Manhattan or an Old-Fashioned.*

Molasses Wine

Rum is the distilled essence of fermented sugar. In this liqueur, this essence is enhanced with the spirit of grapes (in the vermouth) and a wallop of molasses, the corporeal fluid that is left behind when sugar transubstantiates into spirit. The result is wildly pungent and deeply aromatic; it punches up any favorite dark rum drink with its moxie.

MAKES ABOUT 1 QUART

1⅓   cups dark rum (80 proof)

½   cup sweet (red) vermouth (18% ABV)

1   vanilla bean (Madagascar or Bourbon), split

¼   cup dark molasses

1¼   cups Brown Simple Syrup (page 24)

1. Combine the rum, vermouth, vanilla, molasses, and simple syrup in a 1-quart jar.

2. Seal the jar and put it in a cool, dark cabinet until the liquid smells and tastes pleasantly of molasses, 2 to 3 days.

3. Strain the mixture with a mesh strainer into a clean quart jar. Do not push on the solids to extract more liquid.

4. Seal and store in a cool, dark cabinet. Use within 1 year.

Y *Salut!* Try it in a Planter's Punch or Rum and Coke.

Jaggery

Jaggery, the unrefined raw sugar from India, Pakistan, and Sri Lanka, can be made from sugarcane or date palm. Palm jaggery is soft and spreadable and considered the better-tasting variety, although it is rarely found outside of the Indus peninsula. Sugarcane jaggery is commonly available in Indian and Pakistani grocery stores, most often sold in small pyramidal cakes weighing about 1½ ounces each.

Sugarcane jaggery is very sweet and very hard. Because it does not dissolve in alcohol, you will need to dissolve it in water before using it in liqueur production. Jaggery liqueur tastes like rum but is more floral and grassy.

MAKES ABOUT 1 QUART

1 cup water
1 (2-inch) piece fresh ginger, minced
12 ounces solid jaggery (raw Indian sugar), about eight 1½-ounce cakes, cut into small pieces
2 cups dark rum (80 proof)

1. Put the water and ginger in a small saucepan. Bring to a boil over medium heat. Lower the heat to a simmer, add the jaggery, and stir until the jaggery dissolves. Let cool.

2. Combine the jaggery syrup and rum in a 1-quart jar. Stir to combine.

3. Seal the jar and put it in a cool, dark cabinet until the liquid smells and tastes strongly of brown sugar with a hint of ginger, 2 to 3 days.

4. Strain the mixture with a mesh strainer into a clean quart jar. Do not push on the solids to extract more liquid.

5. Seal and store in a cool, dark cabinet. Use within 1 year.

Y *L'chaim!* *Use in any preparation calling for golden rum.*

Coconut-Palm Rum

The raw sugar of the coconut palm was an obscure tropical export not too long ago, but entrepreneurs in Bali have made a thriving business selling granulated palm sugar (they call it evaporated coconut-palm sugar) to health-conscious Americans, touting it as a low-glycemic natural sweetener. You can drink this liqueur for your health, but I encourage you to try it for its beautifully herbal, grassy flavor and rich coconut cream mouthfeel.

MAKES ABOUT 1 QUART

1¼ cups palm sugar
1¼ cups coconut milk
 2 cups dark rum (80 proof)
 1 cup lightly packed sweetened
     flaked coconut

1. Mix the palm sugar and coconut milk in a small saucepan and bring to a boil over medium heat. Let cool.

2. Combine the syrup, rum, and coconut in a half-gallon jar.

3. Seal the jar and put it in a cool, dark cabinet until the liquid smells and tastes strongly of brown sugar and coconut, 3 to 5 days.

4. Put the mixture in the freezer for about 30 minutes. Any fat from the coconut will become solid.

5. Strain the mixture with a mesh strainer into a clean quart jar. Do not push on the solids to extract more liquid.

6. Seal and store in a cool, dark cabinet. Use within 1 year.

Y *Prost!* *A good reason to start drinking Coconut Mojitos (page 243).*

Tippling Brown Sugar

If New England had a signature liqueur, this would have to be it. Redolent with molasses and maple, it is tangy and sweet, like one of those discus-sized molasses cookies baked at the cozy B&B tucked away two blocks off the town green.

MAKES ABOUT 1 QUART

2¼ cups Irish whiskey, Scotch, bourbon, or rye (80 proof)

¼ cup dark molasses

¼ cup pure maple syrup

½ cup Brown Simple Syrup (page 24)

1. Combine the whiskey, molasses, maple syrup, and simple syrup in a 1-quart jar.

2. Seal the jar and put it in a cool, dark cabinet until the liquid smells and tastes strongly of brown sugar, about 1 day. Use within 1 year.

Y **Bottoms Up!** *The definitive liqueur for Scotch and Ginger, and makes a sly addition to a Black Velvet Redux (page 254).*

Sugar in the Raw

Raw turbinado sugar is the most refined of the unrefined sweet-eners. All but a hint of molasses has been removed, and the sugar crystals are uniform and bone-dry. For my taste, turbinado is a bit too tame to be called "raw," so I added a tad more molasses. The result is extremely rounded and pleasant — raw but refined.

MAKES ABOUT 1 QUART

1½ cups turbinado sugar
1 cup water
1¾ cups dark rum (80 proof)
¼ cup dark molasses

1. Mix the turbinado sugar and water in a small saucepan and bring to a boil over medium heat. Let cool.

2. Combine the rum, molasses, and turbinado syrup in a clean quart jar.

3. Seal the jar and put it in a cool, dark cabinet for the flavors to blend, about 1 day. Use within 1 year.

Y **Cheers!** *Use as you would any dark or golden rum.*

Black Sugar

The blackness of this liqueur comes from the deep, dark clouds of coffee and cocoa that invade from within. The intense bitterness of these two ingredients requires a worthy sweet adversary like Caramelized Simple Syrup to set your palate on tilt. The players give their all here, and the result is an utterly adult caffeinated candy.

MAKES ABOUT 1 QUART

2½ cups vodka (80–100 proof)
1 cup (4 ounces) dark-roast coffee beans, cracked
1 cup (4 ounces) cacao nibs
3 cinnamon sticks, cracked
1½ cups Caramelized Simple Syrup (page 24)

1. Combine the vodka, coffee beans, cacao nibs, cinnamon, and simple syrup in a half-gallon jar. Stir to moisten everything.

2. Seal the jar and put it in a cool, dark cabinet until the liquid smells and tastes strongly of coffee and chocolate, about 5 days.

3. Strain the mixture with a mesh strainer into a clean quart jar. Do not push on the solids to extract more liquid.

4. Seal and store in a cool, dark cabinet. Use within 1 year.

....

Y *Sláinte!* Try it to sweeten a Chocolate Martini.

Maple Syrup

There are two main grades of maple syrup in the United States (Canada has a different grading system). The most expensive, grade A, comes in light amber, medium amber, and dark amber; it is the lightest and most nuanced. Grade B is a darker, richer, and more caramelly syrup. That's what you want here.

The flavor of maple combines sweetness, tartness (from malic acid), and aromatics, mostly from proteins and vanillin, a vanilla-tasting by-product of wood. In this delectable liqueur, the taste is underscored by the generic fruit flavor from prunes and a floral hit of vanilla. Serve this liqueur mixed in a warm toddy (a cinnamon stick spiraled with lemon peel makes an excellent swizzle), or as the sweet element in a Rye Old-Fashioned.

MAKES ABOUT 1 QUART

1¾ cups dark rum (80 proof)

1 vanilla bean (Madagascar or Bourbon), split

6 prunes, coarsely chopped

1¾ cups pure maple syrup, preferably grade B

1. Combine the rum, vanilla, prunes, and maple syrup in a 1-quart jar.

2. Seal the jar and put it in a cool, dark cabinet until the liquid smells and tastes strongly of maple with a hint of fruit, 3 to 5 days.

3. Strain the mixture with a mesh strainer into a clean quart jar. Do not push on the solids to extract more liquid.

4. Seal and store in a cool, dark cabinet. Use within 1 year.

Y *L'chaim!* *Get a new perspective with a New-Fashioned Old-Fashioned (page 249).*

INFUSED SPIRITS

TECHNICALLY SPEAKING, FLAVORED VODKAS, GINS, WHISKEYS, AND RUMS do not contain enough sugar to be classified as liqueurs. This lack of sweetness makes them less likely to be served as an aperitif (before a meal) or digestif (after a meal), but it makes them much more versatile as cocktail mixers.

The process of making infused spirits is identical to that of preparing liqueurs. The only difference is that little or no sweetener is added after tincturing. Because no balm of sugar is present to mediate the rough edges of the alcohol, infused spirits tend to be harsher than similarly flavored liqueurs. And yet, compared to the same spirit without flavorings, these tasty liquors feel richer and full-bodied, more substantial than a mere spirit.

Lemon Vodka

The essence of a freshly peeled lemon inspires this vodka to become something more than a mere inebriant. It has a delicate and pungent perfume. The aroma comes from two volatiles in lemon rind: limonene, which gives a general tangy-fruity flavor, and citral, which gives the distinctive aroma of lemon. Lemon vodka has near-infinite uses, from Martinis to Bloody Marys to spiked lemonades.

MAKES 2¾ CUPS

1 fifth (750 ml/3¼ cups)
   vodka (80-100 proof)
   Finely grated zest of 6 lemons

1. Combine the vodka and lemon zest in a 1-quart jar. Stir to moisten the lemon.

2. Seal the jar and put it in a cool, dark cabinet until the liquid smells and tastes strongly of lemon, 2 to 3 days.

3. Strain the mixture with a mesh strainer into a clean quart jar. Do not push on the solids to extract more liquid.

4. Seal and store in a cool, dark cabinet. Use within 1 year.

Y **Cheers!** *Some options: Black Pepper Lemonade (page 242), Archangel (page 247), or Sunshine Cosmo (page 248).*

Green-Apple Vodka

Too often apple flavor is relegated to the woodsy realm of cinnamon and clove, but the clean, crisp, tart pucker of green apple is the essence of freshness. Acknowledging that the apple is a fruit of great refreshment, this spare spirit wipes the palate clean. It is essential for an Appletini.

MAKES 2¾ CUPS

1 fifth (750 ml/3¼ cups)
 vodka (80–100 proof)

1 tablespoon lime juice

3 tart green apples, coarsely grated

1. Combine the vodka, lime juice, and grated apple in a half-gallon jar. Stir to moisten everything.

2. Seal the jar and put it in a cool, dark cabinet until the liquid smells and tastes strongly of apple, 5 to 7 days.

3. Strain the mixture with a mesh strainer into a clean quart jar. Do not push on the solids to extract more liquid.

4. Seal and store in a cool, dark cabinet. Use within 1 year.

Y *L'chaim!* Try it in a Caramel Appletini (page 247).

Ancho Mescal

The glowing, brick red color of ancho chiles in this liquor gives a clue to its intoxicatingly rich earthy aroma and fruity spiciness. This is a full-flavored spirit. A small amount of agave syrup (processed from the same cactus that yields tequila) is added to counteract the bitterness of the chile and oregano. It is surprisingly good in a Bourbon Old-Fashioned, a natural in a Mexican Martini (shake with ice and serve straight up), and a no-brainer for a Bloody Matador (page 241).

MAKES 1 PINT

1 fifth (750 ml/3¼ cups) blanco
    mescal or tequila (80 proof)
¾ cup chopped dried ancho chiles
2 tablespoons dried Mexican oregano
    Finely grated zest of 1 lime
⅓ cup agave syrup

1. Combine the mescal, chiles, oregano, and lime zest in a half-gallon jar. Stir to moisten everything.

2. Seal the jar and put it in a cool, dark cabinet until the liquid smells and tastes strongly of ancho, about 24 hours. *Note the brief infusing time for this recipe.*

3. Strain the mixture with a mesh strainer into a clean quart jar. Do not push on the solids to extract more liquid.

4. Stir in the agave syrup.

5. Seal and store in a cool, dark cabinet. Use within 1 year.

Y *Salut!* Spice up your life with an Ancho Sunset (page 250) or a Capsaicin Cocktail (page 251).

Black Pepper Vodka

Piper nigrum, *the black pepper berry, is harvested green and then blanched for a few seconds to rupture the cells just beneath the skin. These cells house the aromatics in black pepper, releasing a heady combination of piney, citrusy, woody, floral, and spicy components. The flavors in black pepper are so volatile that it only takes hours, rather than days, to infuse them into a neutral spirit. Once trapped by the alcohol, the pepper flavor stays remarkably fresh. Take a sip from a year-old batch of this stuff, and you'd swear the pepper was recently freshly ground. Chug it by the shot, spice up a Bloody Mary, or reinvent the Screwdriver.*

MAKES 1 PINT

1 fifth (750 ml/3¼ cups) vodka (80–100 proof)

½ cup cracked black peppercorns

1. Combine the vodka and peppercorns in a 1-quart jar. Stir to moisten the peppercorns.

2. Seal the jar and put it in a cool, dark cabinet until the liquid smells and tastes strongly of black pepper, 2 to 4 hours. *Note the brief infusing time for this recipe.*

3. Strain the mixture with a mesh strainer into a clean quart jar. Do not push on the solids to extract more liquid.

4. Seal and store in a cool, dark cabinet. Use within 1 year.

Y *Sláinte!* *Zip up your taste buds with a Black Pepper Lemonade (page 242) or a Black Sunburst (page 243).*

Horseradish Schnapps

You need fresh horseradish root for this liquor. Jarred prepared horseradish is too finely grated, which tends to make the spirit overly cloudy. It also contains trace amounts of vinegar, oil, and salt, which would affect the clean, clear flavor.

Whole horseradish root has practically no aroma, but when it is grated, the broken cells produce mustard oil (horseradish and mustard belong to the same botanical family), which irritates your mucous membranes. The membranes weep to rid your system of the irritating oil, producing a cleansing effect throughout your skull. That effect, though moderately painful, is wonderfully refreshing.

MAKES 1 PINT

1   fifth (750 ml/3¼ cups) vodka
     (80-100 proof)
1½ cups coarsely shredded fresh
     horseradish root

1. Combine the vodka and horseradish in a half-gallon jar. Stir to moisten the horseradish.

2. Seal the jar and put it in a cool, dark cabinet until the liquid smells and tastes strongly of horseradish, 2 to 4 hours.

3. Strain the mixture with a mesh strainer lined with several layers of dampened cheesecloth into a clean quart jar. Do not push on the solids to extract more liquid.

4. Seal and store in a cool, dark cabinet. Use within 1 year.

NOTE: The liqueur will precipitate small bits of horseradish as it sits. These are not harmful, but you might find them unattractive. To cleanse your Horseradish Schnapps, follow the directions for clarifying (see page 8).

🍸 *Santé!* *Obviously this is the vodka of choice for Bloody Marys (try the Classic Bloody Mary on page 241). Also makes a lethal shooter.*

Minted Bourbon

The first mention of the mint julep (1803) describes a drink served at the Old White, the main building of The Greenbrier resort in White Sulphur Springs, West Virginia. It is a classic "smash," a style of cocktail in which herbs are muddled, or smashed, in the bottom of a shaker or glass, mixed with sugar syrup and booze, then poured over ice. Minted Bourbon is nothing more or less than a shortcut to the historic cocktail.

MAKES 2½ CUPS

1 fifth (750 ml/3¼ cups) bourbon (80 proof)

3 cups finely chopped fresh mint

⅓ cup Simple Syrup (page 24)

1. Combine the bourbon and mint in a half-gallon jar. Stir to moisten the mint.

2. Seal the jar and put it in a cool, dark cabinet until the liquid smells and tastes strongly of mint, 2 to 3 days.

3. Strain the mixture with a mesh strainer into a clean quart jar. Do not push on the solids to extract more liquid.

4. Stir in the simple syrup.

5. Seal and store in a cool, dark cabinet. Use within 1 year.

Y *Prost!* *Pour over crushed ice and garnish with a sprig of mint for an instantaneous Mint Julep.*

Orange Rye

Compared to the caramel silkiness of many bourbons and Scotches, rye whiskey is downright coarse. Slightly bitter, with its flavors not quite integrated, to my palate rye comes off chewy, more like food than drink. Adding a hint of orange seems to smooth everything out. The infusion of citrus makes this rye a natural in an Old-Fashioned.

MAKES 1 PINT

1 fifth (750 ml/3¼ cups) rye whiskey (80 proof)

1½ cups finely grated fresh orange zest

¼ cup Simple Syrup (page 24)

1. Combine the rye and orange peel in a half-gallon jar. Stir to moisten the peel.

2. Seal the jar and put it in a cool, dark cabinet until the liquid smells and tastes strongly of orange, 2 to 3 days.

3. Strain the mixture with a mesh strainer into a clean quart jar. Do not push on the solids to extract more liquid.

4. Stir in the simple syrup.

5. Seal and store in a cool, dark cabinet. Use within 1 year.

Y *Skål! Looking for something different? Try a B-52 (page 239), an Apertivo (page 245), or a Prunelle Martini (page 248).*

Cucumber Gin

All gins are flavored with aromatic herbs, spices, and vegetables. The Dutch style enhances the effect of those aromatics by adding more of them in an extra distillation. This last pass through the still boosts the flavor profile considerably, creating gins with overtly floral or vegetal aromas. One of the most delightful of these flavors is cucumber. Hendrick's, a very flavorful Dutch-style gin, is known for its cucumbery profile. This infused spirit is a tribute to that refreshing Hendrick's persona.

MAKES 3 CUPS

2   medium English cucumbers, coarsely shredded
½   teaspoon coarse sea salt
1   fifth (750 ml/3¼ cups) Dutch-style gin (80 proof)
¼   cup dry vermouth (18% ABV)

1. Mix the cucumber and salt in a small bowl and squeeze with your hands for a few minutes. Once the cucumber has released a good amount of liquid, combine the mixture with the gin and vermouth in a half-gallon jar.

2. Seal the jar and shake briefly. Put it in a cool, dark cabinet until the liquid smells and tastes strongly of cucumber, 2 to 3 days.

3. Strain the mixture with a mesh strainer lined with several layers of dampened cheesecloth into a clean quart jar. Do not push on the solids to extract more liquid.

4. Seal and store in a cool, dark cabinet. Use within 1 year.

Y *Bottoms Up!* *Amazing Gimlet — naturally. Cucumber Martini I (page 247) — absolutely brilliant!*

Vanilla Vodka

Vanilla selflessly donates its quiet sophistication to whatever it touches. Innocently sweet in a custardy eggnog, it can also be exotic, lending a jungle floral fragrance to mango or coconut liqueur, or it can soothe and modulate the harsh notes of dark-roast coffee. This all-purpose flavored vodka is the perfect vehicle for all of that and more.

MAKES ABOUT 1 QUART

1 fifth (750 ml/3¼ cups) vodka (80–100 proof)

2 vanilla beans (Madagascar or Bourbon), halved and split

¼ cup Simple Syrup (page 24)

1. Combine the vodka and vanilla in a half-gallon jar and stir.

2. Seal the jar and put it in a cool, dark cabinet until the liquid smells and tastes strongly of vanilla, 2 to 3 days.

3. Strain the mixture with a mesh strainer into a clean quart jar. Do not push on the solids to extract more liquid.

4. Stir in the simple syrup.

5. Seal and store in a cool, dark cabinet. Use within 1 year.

Y **Cheers!** *The ultimate vodka for a White Russian.*

Coconut Rum

Of all the coconut-rum mixtures in this book (this one brings the total to an even half dozen) this is the simplest, cleanest, and most versatile. It packs unadulterated coconut flavor. Coconut comes in several forms: fresh, dried shredded, and dried flaked. Although flaked coconut is the most processed, it yields the fullest coconut flavor to liqueurs. Because it is already sweetened, no added sugar syrup is necessary.

MAKES 1 PINT

1 fifth (750 ml/3¼ cups)
   light rum (80 proof)
3 cups lightly packed sweetened
   flaked coconut

1. Combine the rum and coconut in a half-gallon jar. Stir to moisten the coconut flakes.

2. Seal the jar and put it in a cool, dark cabinet until the liquid smells and tastes strongly of coconut, 2 to 3 days.

3. Strain the mixture with a mesh strainer into a clean quart jar. Do not push on the solids to extract more liquid.

4. Seal and store in a cool, dark cabinet. Use within 1 year.

Y L'chaim! Makes a patently delicious Daiquiri.

Lemon Drop
(Copycat Limoncello),
page 60

Summer Cantaloupe,
page 68

Angelica
(Copycat Chartreuse),
page 116

Pomegranate
Negroni,
page 255

Chocolate Xander,
page 240

New-Fashioned
Old-Fashioned,
page 249

3

Cocktail Hour

Cocktail Hour

It wasn't until the beginning of the nineteenth century that the practice of mixing spirits into cocktails became popular in Europe and the Americas. Before then wine, beer, and spirits were consumed regularly, but almost never in combination with other ingredients and rarely adorned with anything more elaborate than ice. To my mind, that is still the best way to appreciate the true nature of finely made alcohol, but it's not the only way.

Cocktails by their very nature are frippery — serious fun whose sole purpose is to delight and entertain — but the practice of mixing cocktails is anything but flippant. There are standard methods that almost all cocktails adhere to, and they have not changed since the dawn of mixology.

The original cocktail, described first in 1806, was a mixture of spirits, sugar, water, and bitters. This simple combination became known as an Old-Fashioned, to differentiate it from the more complex newfangled concoctions that came into vogue at the end of the nineteenth century.

Today, cocktail websites list a mind-boggling assortment of mixed drinks, often without rhyme or reason. The field can seem unnavigable, but except for a few dozen outliers, five basic cocktail templates encompass all those thousands (more or less). These basic types can be endlessly modified with any number of garnishes and additional ingredients, as well as techniques such as blending and layering, or even eye-popping special effects, like flaming.

As the author of The Bar-Tender's Guide *(also known as* How to Mix Drinks *or* The Bon-Vivant's Companion*), Jerry Thomas (1830–1885) is considered the father of mixology. His book, the first of its kind published in the United States, codified cocktail recipes. Here he mixes his signature concoction, the Blue Blazer.*

Five Basic Cocktail Types

SPIRITS + SUGAR + FLAVORING

Old-Fashioned, Mint Julep, Sazerac

SPIRITS + VERMOUTH OR LIQUEUR + (OPTIONAL FLAVORING)

Martini, Manhattan, Cosmopolitan, Negroni, Rusty Nail, Stinger, White Lady, Tuxedo, Black Russian, French Connection, Godfather/ Godmother, Kir

SPIRITS + SOUR + SUGAR + (OPTIONAL FLAVORING)

Sidecar, Margarita, Daiquiri, Mojito, Caipirinha, Whiskey Sour, Mai Tai, Long Island Iced Tea, Kamikaze

SPIRITS + BEVERAGE (JUICE, SODA, COFFEE, BEER, WINE) + FLAVORING

Bloody Mary, Screwdriver, Gin and Tonic, Gin Fizz, John Collins, Planter's Punch, Cuba Libre, Mimosa, Piña Colada, Moscow Mule, French 75, Harvey Wallbanger, Horse's Neck, Singapore Sling, Tequila Sunrise, Irish Coffee

SPIRITS + CREAM OR EGG + FLAVORING

Alexander, Porto Flip, Ramos Fizz, Grasshopper

Completing the Cocktail

Of the four basic constituents of cocktails — spirits, sugar, water, and bitters — we dealt with the first two in part 1 (see pages 1–27). Now let's talk about water and bitters.

Why Add Water?

Water is the secret ingredient in just about every cocktail. Whether it is in the form of ice, seltzer, juice, or a splash of branch water, H_2O mixes easily with ethanol (CH_3CH_2OH), which is the main alcohol in distilled spirits.

When first combined in a mixed drink, the water forms visible waves due to the difference in density between ethanol and alcohol. Eventually the two combine completely, lowering the percentage of alcohol (ABV) in the drink and allowing your palate to pick up more of the aromatic flavor molecules in the spirit.

Although this phenomenon is noticeable in all cocktails, it is most pronounced in simple mixtures like Scotch on the rocks or a dry martini. A dry martini (one with barely a whisper of vermouth) is little more than gin or vodka mixed with ice. The ice chills the booze, but more important, it gradually melts into water, which bonds with the alcohol and releases its innate flavors. That is why it is necessary to let a martini rest for a minute during shaking or stirring, to give the ice a little more time to turn into water.

What about Bitters?

Bitters are concentrated flavoring agents used to season cocktails. As their name implies, they typically contain a bittering ingredient, most commonly cinchona bark (quinine) or gentian root; others include angelica, artichoke leaf, bitter orange, thistle leaves, wormwood, and yarrow.

The mixtures that are now sold as cocktail bitters were originally patent medicines. For example, Angostura bitters was first compounded as a treatment for seasickness and stomach distress. Originating in Venezuela in 1824, it was used as a medicine by the British Royal Navy, administered in gin. Pink gin became a popular nineteenth-century digestif cocktail in the United Kingdom.

The addition of bitters is one of the elements that defines early cocktail formulas, and rightly so. It forms the fourth leg in the flavor platform of cocktails. Distilled spirits naturally have a balance of sugar, acid, protein, and salt, from the wine and beer used for distillation. Bitterness is the only major taste that is missing. Bitters are not included in all cocktail recipes, and are more common in brown liquor mixtures like Old-Fashioneds and Manhattans.

WHYS & WHEREFORES OF BARWARE

Cocktails can also be categorized by the glasses in which they are traditionally served.

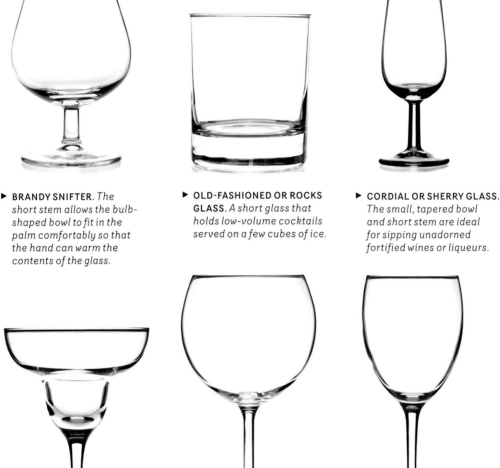

▶ **BRANDY SNIFTER.** *The short stem allows the bulb-shaped bowl to fit in the palm comfortably so that the hand can warm the contents of the glass.*

▶ **OLD-FASHIONED OR ROCKS GLASS.** *A short glass that holds low-volume cocktails served on a few cubes of ice.*

▶ **CORDIAL OR SHERRY GLASS.** *The small, tapered bowl and short stem are ideal for sipping unadorned fortified wines or liqueurs.*

▶ **MARGARITA GLASS.** *The "classic" design is the sort of champagne glass known as a coupe but it's hard to pin down why it is pre-ferred. It could be that the wide rim holds more salt and the two-tiered shape gives volume while allowing the salt rim to stay dry.*

▶ **GOBLET OR WINEGLASS.** *The spherical or tapering bowl captures the aroma of a fine wine or liqueur; the stem allows the drinker to grasp the glass without touching the bowl.*

▶ **MUG.** *This thick-walled cylinder has a handle for hot drinks.*

▶ **COLLINS GLASS.** *The tall narrow column highlights drinks mixed with carbonated water.*

▶ **HIGHBALL GLASS.** *This all-purpose tapered column is suitable for many mixed drinks.*

▶ **CHAMPAGNE FLUTE.** *The elongated narrow bowl showcases the bubbles, and the long stem allows the drinker to grasp the glass without touching the bowl and warming the bubbly.*

▶ **COCKTAIL GLASS.** *The long stem allows the drinker to hold the glass without warming the contents, while the wide, cone-shaped bowl shows off garniture.*

▶ **SHOT GLASS.** *Available in many shapes, this 1- to 4-ounce glass is used for quick gulps of straight spirits or for measuring spirits for mixed drinks.*

Mix It Up!

The collection of cocktails that follows is by no means exhaustive or intended as a mixology encyclopedia, but is meant to illustrate the versatility of making mixed drinks with liqueurs. In these recipes, liqueurs replace the spirit and the sugar that make up more traditional concoctions. They are arranged by basic cocktail recipe as follows:

ALEXANDER

LIQUEUR SPIRIT + CREAM

Originally a mixture of gin, créme de cacao, and cream, now more commonly made with brandy, the name comes from the New York bartender Troy Alexander, who invented the creamy white cocktail to honor Phoebe Snow, a fictional advertising figure for the Delaware, Lackawanna & Western Railroad. Dressed in snow white, she represented the cleanliness of anthracite-powered locomotives, were claimed to be as pure as freshly fallen snow.

B-52

SHOT GLASS, SWIZZLE STICK

- ½ oz Double Shot (page 168)
- ½ oz Orange Rye (page 225)
- ½ oz Irish Cream (page 188), chilled

Mix the Double Shot and Orange Rye together. Spoon the Irish Cream on top to float.

Banshee

CHILLED COCKTAIL GLASS, COCKTAIL SHAKER

- Ice cubes
- 1 oz Coco-Loco (page 182)
- 1 oz Tropical Banana (page 39)
- 2 oz light cream
- Sprinkle of cocoa powder

Fill shaker with ice cubes. Add Coco-Loco, Tropical Banana, and light cream; shake well. Wait 1 minute, shake again, strain into glass. Garnish with a sprinkle of cocoa powder.

Bourbon Milk Punch

HIGHBALL GLASS, SWIZZLE STICK

- 4 oz milk
- 2 oz Corny Corn "Liquor" (page 91)
- Pinch of ground cinnamon
- 2-3 ice cubes
- Cinnamon stick

Pour Corny Corn "Liquor" and milk into glass; add cinnamon and stir. Add ice cubes. Garnish with cinnamon stick.

Brandy Al

CHILLED COCKTAIL GLASS, COCKTAIL SHAKER

- Ice cubes
- 1 oz Coco-Loco (page 182)
- 1 oz brandy
- 1 oz heavy cream
- Freshly grated nutmeg

Fill shaker with ice cubes. Add Coco-Loco, brandy, and cream and shake vigorously; strain into glass. Garnish with nutmeg.

Chocolate Xander, 240

Brandy Coquito

CHILLED COCKTAIL GLASS, COCKTAIL SHAKER

  Ice cubes
2 oz Eggnog (page 191)
2 oz coconut milk
  Pinch of ground cinnamon

Fill shaker with ice. Add Eggnog and
coconut milk; shake vigorously. Strain
into glass. Garnish with cinnamon.

Chocolate Xander

CHILLED COCKTAIL GLASS, COCKTAIL SHAKER

  Ice cubes
2 oz Coco-Loco (page 182)
1 oz light cream
  Freshly grated nutmeg

Fill shaker with ice. Add Coco-Loco and cream
and shake. Wait for 1 minute; shake again;
strain into glass. Garnish with nutmeg.

Chocolate-Caramel-Hazelnut Espresso

ESPRESSO CUP, DEMITASSE SPOON

1 oz Caramelized Simple Syrup
  (page 24)
2 oz freshly brewed espresso
2 oz Chocolate Hazelnut (page 137)
1–2 tbsp whipped cream

Mix the simple syrup into the espresso until
dissolved. Add the Chocolate Hazelnut and
stir once. Spoon whipped cream on top.

Creamy Irish Coffee

MUG

2 oz Irish Cream (page 188)
4 oz hot freshly brewed coffee
1 tbsp whipped cream

Combine Irish Cream and coffee in the
mug; stir. Garnish with whipped cream.

Hazelnut Coffee

COFFEE CUP

2 oz Coffee Nut (page 172)
4 oz freshly brewed coffee
1 oz heavy cream
  Sprinkle of ground cinnamon

Combine Coffee Nut and coffee in
the mug; stir. Spoon the cream on
top. Garnish with cinnamon.

Mocha Nut

COFFEE CUP

2 oz Coco-Loco (page 182)
2 oz Chocolate Hazelnut (page 137)
4 oz freshly brewed espresso
1 oz heavy cream
  Sprinkle of ground cinnamon

Combine the Coco-Loco, Chocolate Hazelnut,
and espresso in the cup; stir. Spoon the
cream on top. Garnish with cinnamon.

Oaxaca Eggnog

CHILLED COCKTAIL GLASS, COCKTAIL SHAKER

1 tsp cinnamon sugar
  Ice cubes
2 oz Eggnog (page 191)
1 oz reposado tequila
  Cinnamon stick

Wet rim of glass and coat with sugar. Fill
shaker with ice; add Eggnog and tequila;
shake. Wait for 1 minute; shake again; strain
into glass. Garnish with cinnamon stick.

Streamlined White Russian

CHILLED COCKTAIL GLASS, COCKTAIL SHAKER

  Ice cubes
4 oz White Russian (page 190)
  Freshly grated nutmeg

Fill shaker with ice; add White Russian
and shake. Wait for 1 minute; shake again;
strain into glass. Garnish with nutmeg.

BLOODY MARY

LIQUEUR SPIRIT + VEGETABLE JUICE

A mixture of vodka, velvet-thick tomato juice, and tangy condiments (Worcestershire, horseradish, hot pepper sauce, you name it), the Bloody Mary is a cocktail on the verge of turning into a food. Its edibility is substantial enough that you could even call a Bloody Mary and a cup of coffee the equivalent of brunch, give or take a serving of eggs Benedict.

Bloody Maria
HIGHBALL GLASS, SWIZZLE STICK

1	tsp coarsely ground black pepper
	Ice cubes
1	oz Sweet-Heat Firewater (page 90)
1	oz Lime Agave (page 63)
4	oz vegetable cocktail juice (V8)
1	fresh jalapeño chile
	Wedge of lime

Wet the rim of the glass and coat with the pepper. Fill the glass with ice. Add the Sweet Heat Firewater, Lime Agave, and juice; stir. Garnish with jalapeño chile and lime wedge.

Bloody Matador
HIGHBALL GLASS, SWIZZLE STICK

	Ice cubes
2	oz Ancho Mescal (page 220)
4	oz vegetable cocktail juice (V8)
	Wedge of lime

Fill glass with ice. Add Ancho Mescal and juice; stir. Garnish with lime wedge.

Classic Bloody Mary
HIGHBALL GLASS, SWIZZLE STICK

	Ice cubes
2	oz Horseradish Schnapps (page 223)
4	oz vegetable cocktail juice (V8)
	Wedge of lime

Fill glass with ice cubes. Add Horseradish Schnapps and juice; stir. Garnish with lime wedge.

Classic Bloody Mary

Red Skies at Night
HIGHBALL GLASS, SWIZZLE STICK

    Ice cubes
2 oz Red Lightning (page 92)
4 oz tomato juice
    Wedge of lime

Fill glass with ice. Add Red Lightning and juice; stir. Garnish with lime wedge.

Smokin' Mary
HIGHBALL GLASS, SWIZZLE STICK

    Ice cubes
2 oz Smokin' (page 178)
4 oz vegetable cocktail juice (V8)
    Dash of chipotle hot sauce
    Wedge of lime

Fill glass with ice. Add Smokin', juice, and hot sauce; stir. Garnish with lime wedge.

COOLER

LIQUEUR SPIRIT + JUICE + SODA

As the name implies, coolers, with a hint of fruit juice, a hit of alcohol, and a refreshing effervescence from soda water, are the summertime libation of choice for most tipplers. These easy-to-love thirst quenchers are ubiquitous, encompassing a wide variety of cocktails, including Collinses, Spritzers, and Mojitos.

Black Pepper Lemonade
HIGHBALL GLASS, SWIZZLE STICK

3 ice cubes
1 oz Black Pepper Vodka (page 222)
1 oz Lemon Vodka (page 218)
2 oz Simple Syrup (page 24)
1 oz fresh lemon juice
4 oz seltzer
    Wedge of lemon

Fill glass with ice. Add the Black Pepper Vodka, Lemon Vodka, simple syrup, lemon juice, and seltzer; stir. Garnish with lemon wedge.

End-of-Summer Cocktail, 243

Black Sunburst

HIGHBALL GLASS, SWIZZLE STICK

- 3 ice cubes
- 2 oz Black Pepper Vodka (page 222)
- 2 oz Simple Syrup (page 24)
- 4 oz fresh orange juice
- 4 oz seltzer
  Wedge of lemon

Put the ice in the glass. Add the Black Pepper Vodka, simple syrup, orange juice, and seltzer; stir. Garnish with lemon wedge.

Blushing Spritzer

WINEGLASS, SWIZZLE STICK

- 1 ice cube
- 1 oz Ruby Slippers (page 161)
- 4 oz Chardonnay
- 4 oz seltzer
- 3 rose petals or 6 pomegranate seeds

Put the ice cube in the glass. Add the Ruby Slippers, Chardonnay, and seltzer; stir. Garnish with rose petals or pomegranate seeds.

Coconut Mojito

HIGHBALL GLASS, COCKTAIL SHAKER

- Ice cubes
- 2 oz Coconut-Palm Rum (page 210)
- 1½ oz coconut water
- ¾ oz fresh lime juice
- 3 oz seltzer
  Slice of lime

Fill shaker and glass with ice. Pour the Coconut-Palm Rum, coconut water, and lime juice into the shaker; shake vigorously; strain into glass. Pour seltzer into glass. Garnish with lime wedge.

Cola Coffee

HIGHBALL GLASS, COCKTAIL SHAKER

- Ice cubes
- 1 oz Toasted Tropics (page 148)
- 1 oz Double Shot (page 168)
- 1 oz pineapple juice
- 3 oz cola
  Wedge of lime

Fill shaker with ice and put 2 cubes in glass. Pour the Toasted Tropics, Double Shot, and pineapple juice into the shaker; shake vigorously; strain into glass. Pour cola into glass. Garnish with lime wedge.

Electric Raspberry Lemonade

HIGHBALL GLASS, COCKTAIL SHAKER

- Ice cubes
- 2 oz Raspberry Rose (page 156)
- 1 oz sour mix
- 4 oz seltzer
- 3 fresh raspberries
  Slice of lemon

Fill the shaker with ice; put 2 cubes in the glass. Add the Raspberry Rose and sour mix to the shaker and shake; strain into glass. Pour seltzer into glass. Garnish with raspberries and lemon slice.

End-of-Summer Cocktail

OLD-FASHIONED GLASS, COCKTAIL SHAKER

- Ice cubes
- 3 oz Minty Melon (page 70)
- ½ oz fresh lime juice
- 3 oz seltzer
  Fresh mint sprig

Fill the shaker with ice and put 2 cubes in the glass. Add the Minty Melon and lime juice to the shaker and shake; strain into the glass. Fill the glass with seltzer. Garnish with mint.

Flaming Lemonade

OLD-FASHIONED GLASS, COCKTAIL SHAKER

	Ice cubes
3	oz Sweet-Heat Firewater (page 90)
½	oz fresh lemon juice
1	tablespoon honey
1	oz lemon-lime soda
	Slice of lemon

Fill the shaker with ice and put 2 cubes in the glass. Add the Sweet Heat Firewater, lemon juice, and honey to the shaker and shake; strain into the glass. Fill the glass with soda. Garnish with lemon slice.

Hawaiian Mojito

CHILLED COCKTAIL GLASS, MUDDLER, COCKTAIL SHAKER

6	fresh mint leaves
	Ice cubes
3	oz Toasted Tropics (page 148)
½	oz fresh lime juice
3	oz lemon-lime soda
	Wedge of lime

Muddle the mint leaves in the shaker, then fill with ice. Add the Toasted Tropics and lime juice to shaker and shake vigorously; strain into glass. Pour the soda into the glass. Squeeze the lime into the drink and drop it in the glass.

Hawaiian Punch

HIGHBALL GLASS, SWIZZLE STICK

	Crushed ice
2	oz Sweet Almond (page 134)
1	oz Pom-Pom (page 67)
2	oz fresh orange juice
2	oz lemon-lime soda
	Twist of orange peel

Fill the glass with crushed ice. Add the Sweet Almond, Pom-Pom, orange juice, and soda to the glass and stir. Garnish with orange peel.

Lemon Tree

HIGHBALL GLASS, COCKTAIL SHAKER

	Ice cubes
2	oz Lemon Drop (page 60)
	Dash of juniper bitters
1	oz fresh lemon juice
3 to 4	oz seltzer
	Fresh mint sprig

Fill the shaker with ice and put 2 cubes in the glass. Add the Lemon Drop, bitters, and lemon juice to the shaker and shake; strain into the glass. Fill the glass with seltzer. Garnish with mint.

Madras Cocktail

OLD-FASHIONED GLASS, SWIZZLE STICK

2	ice cubes
2	oz Cranberry Clarity (page 50)
3	oz fresh grapefruit juice
	Splash of tonic
	Twist of grapefruit peel

Put the ice cubes in the glass. Add the Cranberry Clarity, grapefruit juice, and tonic; stir. Garnish with peel.

Orange Blossom Mimosa

CHILLED FLUTE, SWIZZLE STICK

1	oz Orange Blossom (page 162)
1	oz fresh orange juice
4	oz chilled Champagne
	Small strawberry

Pour the Orange Blossom, orange juice, and Champagne into the glass; stir. Garnish with strawberry.

MANHATTAN

LIQUEUR SPIRIT + VERMOUTH OR AROMATIC LIQUEUR + BITTERS

Originally mixed from rye, sweet vermouth, and bitters, the Manhattan is now more commonly made with bourbon rather than rye, although my preference remains with the original whiskey. It is considered by many to be the definitive cocktail for its streamlined simplicity and flavorful balance. In many of the recipes given here, the vermouth is amended or replaced by an aromatic liqueur.

Apertivo

CHILLED COCKTAIL GLASS,
COCKTAIL SHAKER

> Ice cubes
> 2 oz Orange Rye (page 225)
> 2 oz Anisette (page 107)
> 6 dashes of orange bitters
> Twist of orange peel

Fill the shaker with ice. Add the Orange Rye, Anisette, and bitters; shake. Wait for 1 minute; shake again; strain into the glass. Garnish with peel.

Autumn Leaves

CHILLED COCKTAIL GLASS,
COCKTAIL SHAKER

> Ice cubes
> 2 oz Apple Brandy (page 32)
> 1 oz rye whiskey
> 1 oz sweet (red) vermouth
> Dash of Angostura bitters
> Cinnamon stick

Fill the shaker with ice. Add the Apple Brandy, whiskey, vermouth, and bitters; shake. Wait for 1 minute; shake again; strain into the glass. Garnish with cinnamon stick.

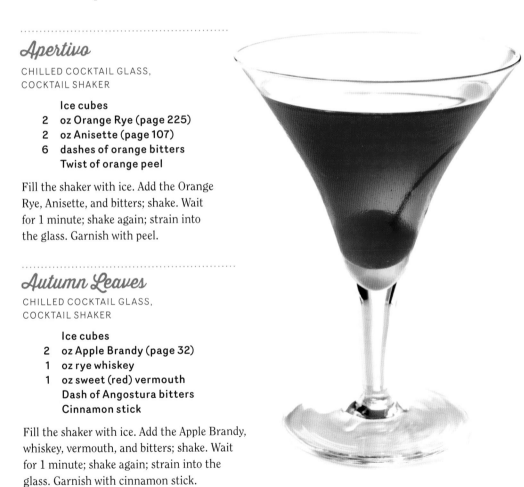

Manhattan Streamlined, 246

Bittersweet Sour Cherry

CHILLED COCKTAIL GLASS, COCKTAIL SHAKER

Ice cubes
2 oz Sweet-and-Sour Cherry (page 44)
1 oz sweet (red) vermouth
2 dashes of Peychaud's bitters
Fresh tarragon sprig

Fill the shaker with ice. Add the Sweet-and-Sour Cherry, vermouth, and bitters; shake. Wait for 1 minute; shake again; strain into the glass. Garnish with tarragon.

Glazed Wild Turkey

OLD-FASHIONED GLASS, SWIZZLE STICK

1 ice cube
2 oz Wild Turkey bourbon
1 oz Caramel Candy (page 143)
1 or 2 dashes orange bitters
Peach or apricot slice

Put the ice cube in the glass. Add the Wild Turkey, Carmel Candy, and bitters; stir. Garnish with fruit.

Golden Caipirinha

CHILLED COCKTAIL GLASS, COCKTAIL SHAKER

Ice cubes
3 oz Gingergold (page 82)
½ oz fresh lemon juice
Dash of cardamom bitters
Strip of yellow bell pepper

Fill the shaker with ice. Add the Gingergold, lemon juice, and bitters; shake. Wait for 1 minute; shake again; strain into the glass. Garnish with bell pepper.

Manhattan Rustico

CHILLED COCKTAIL GLASS, COCKTAIL SHAKER

Ice cubes
2 oz Sweet-Pepper Surprise (page 80)
1 oz rye whiskey
Dash of Angostura bitters
Strip of red bell pepper

Fill the shaker with ice. Add the Sweet-Pepper Surprise, rye whiskey, and bitters; shake. Wait for 1 minute; shake again; strain into the glass. Garnish with bell pepper.

Manhattan Streamlined

CHILLED COCKTAIL GLASS, COCKTAIL SHAKER

Ice cubes
2 oz Hop Blossom (page 163)
1 oz sweet (red) vermouth
Maraschino cherry

Fill the shaker with ice. Add the Hop Blossom and vermouth; shake. Wait for 1 minute; shake again; strain into the glass. Garnish with cherry.

MARTINI

LIQUEUR SPIRIT + ICE + VERMOUTH OR AROMATIC LIQUEUR (OPTIONAL)

The bone-dry martini served in most bars has reduced this elegant drink to a glass of iced booze. The original comprised nearly equal parts aromatic gin and aromatic wine (vermouth); perfume was its raison d'être. Now you can resurrect the martini to its original fragrant perfection.

Allied Forces

CHILLED COCKTAIL GLASS, COCKTAIL SHAKER

> Ice cubes
> 2 oz Dutch-style gin
> 1 oz Herb-Santé (page 108)
> ½ oz Caraway (page 120)
> Slice of orange

Fill the shaker with ice. Add the gin, Herb-Santé, and Caraway; shake. Wait for 1 minute; shake again; strain into the glass. Garnish with orange slice.

Cucumber Martini

Archangel

CHILLED COCKTAIL GLASS, COCKTAIL SHAKER

> Ice cubes
> 2 oz Lemon Vodka (page 218)
> 2 oz Cool as a Cuke (page 98)
> 1 (1-inch) piece cucumber, finely chopped
> Twist of lemon peel

Fill the shaker with ice. Add the Lemon Vodka, Cool as a Cuke, and chopped cucumber; shake. Wait for 1 minute; shake again; strain into the glass. Garnish with lemon twist.

Caramel Appletini

CHILLED COCKTAIL GLASS, COCKTAIL SHAKER

> Ice cubes
> 1 oz Caramel Apple (page 206)
> 2 oz Green-Apple Vodka (page 219)
> Thin wedge of green apple

Fill the shaker with ice. Add the Caramel Apple, Green Apple Vodka, and chopped cucumber; shake. Wait for 1 minute; shake again; strain into the glass. Garnish with apple slice.

Cucumber Martini 1

CHILLED COCKTAIL GLASS, COCKTAIL SHAKER

> Ice cubes
> 3 oz Cucumber Gin (page 226)
> 3 paper-thin cucumber slices

Fill the shaker with ice. Add the Cucumber Gin; shake. Wait for 1 minute; shake again; strain into the glass. Garnish with cucumber slices.

Cucumber Martini 2

CHILLED COCKTAIL GLASS, COCKTAIL SHAKER

Ice cubes
3 oz Cool as a Cuke (page 98)
3 paper-thin cucumber slices

Fill the shaker with ice. Add the Cool as a Cuke; shake. Wait for 1 minute; shake again; strain into the glass. Garnish with cucumber slices.

Elk

CHILLED COCKTAIL GLASS, COCKTAIL SHAKER

Ice cubes
1 oz Prunelle (page 73)
2 oz dry gin
Slice of orange

Fill the shaker with ice. Add the Prunelle and gin; shake. Wait for 1 minute; shake again; strain into the glass. Garnish with orange slice.

Flowering Martini

CHILLED COCKTAIL GLASS, COCKTAIL SHAKER

Ice cubes
3 oz Dutch-style gin
½ oz Elderflower Blush (page 164)
Dash of orange bitters
Twist of lemon peel
3 rose petals (optional)

Fill the shaker with ice. Add the gin, Elderflower Blush, and bitters; shake. Wait for 1 minute; shake again; strain into the glass. Garnish with lemon twist and rose petals.

Mango Martini

CHILLED COCKTAIL GLASS, COCKTAIL SHAKER

Ice cubes
1 oz Mango Twist (page 76)
2 oz reposado tequila
Twist of lemon peel

Fill the shaker with ice. Add the Mango Twist and tequila; shake. Wait for 1 minute; shake again; strain into the glass. Garnish with lemon twist.

Prunelle Martini

CHILLED COCKTAIL GLASS, COCKTAIL SHAKER

Ice cubes
1½ oz Prunelle (page 73)
1½ oz Orange Rye (page 225)
Dash of orange bitters
Twist of orange peel

Fill the shaker with ice. Add the Prunelle, Orange Rye, and bitters; shake. Wait for 1 minute; shake again; strain into the glass. Garnish with orange twist.

Sunshine Cosmo

CHILLED COCKTAIL GLASS, COCKTAIL SHAKER

Ice cubes
2 oz Pure Gold (page 159)
1 oz Lemon Vodka (page 218)
1½ oz fresh orange juice
Twist of orange peel

Fill the shaker with ice. Add the Pure Gold, Lemon Vodka, and orange juice; shake. Wait for 1 minute; shake again; strain into the glass. Garnish with orange twist.

Volcano

CHILLED COCKTAIL GLASS, COCKTAIL SHAKER

1 teaspoon smoked salt
Ice cubes
1 oz Smokin' (page 178)
2 oz blanco tequila
Dash of mole bitters
Fresh serrano chile

Wet the rim of the glass and coat with salt. Fill the shaker with ice. Add the Smokin', tequila, and bitters; shake. Wait for 1 minute; shake again; strain into the glass. Garnish with chile.

OLD-FASHIONED

LIQUEUR SPIRIT + BITTERS

The original cocktail, and by far the most basic, the simple recipe for an Old-Fashioned — whiskey, sugar, and bitters — is beautifully complete and satisfying. Its flavor balance of savory sweetness with a hint of bitter is a standard template for all other types of mixed drinks.

Brandy Sazerac

OLD-FASHIONED GLASS

Ice cubes
Splash of Herb-Santé (page 108)
2 oz Aphrodite (page 121)
3 dashes of Peychaud's bitters
Twist of lemon peel

Fill glass with ice; wait 2 minutes. Dump out the ice; swirl the Herb-Santé in the chilled glass and pour it out. Pour the Aphrodite and bitters into the glass. Rub the lemon peel on the rim of the glass and add it for garnish.

New-Fashioned Old-Fashioned

OLD-FASHIONED GLASS, SWIZZLE STICK

Crushed ice
2 oz Hop Blossom (page 163)
1 oz Maple Syrup (page 214)
Twist of orange peel

Fill the glass with crushed ice. Add the Hop Blossom and Maple Syrup; stir. Garnish with orange twist.

Rooted Old-Fashioned

OLD-FASHIONED GLASS,
MUDDLER, SWIZZLE STICK

1 orange slice
Tiny pinch of smoked salt
2 oz Rüt (page 83)
Dash of bitters, such as Angostura
1 or 2 ice cubes

Put the orange slice and salt in the glass and crush with muddler. Add the Rüt and bitters; stir. Add the ice cubes.

New-Fashioned Old-Fashioned

SCREWDRIVER

LIQUEUR SPIRIT + FRUIT JUICE

The fruity version of a Blood Mary, this is the other brunchtime beverage. More refreshing and less filling, screwdrivers are most typically made with orange juice, but, as the following few recipes confirm, any fruit juice is delicious.

Ancho Sunset

HIGHBALL GLASS, SWIZZLE STICK

Ice cubes
2 oz Ancho Mescal (page 220)
4 oz fresh orange juice
Twist of orange peel

Fill the glass with ice. Add the Ancho Mescal and orange juice; stir. Garnish with orange twist.

Coconut Mai Tai

HIGHBALL GLASS, SWIZZLE STICK

Ice cubes
2 oz Coconut Date (page 71)
2 oz Dark and Stormy Pineapple (page 74)
2 oz fresh orange juice
Splash of Pom-Pom (page 67) or grenadine
Pitted date

Fill the glass with ice. Add the Coconut Date, Dark and Stormy Pineapple, orange juice, and Pom-Pom or grenadine; stir. Garnish with date.

Kiwi Flower Crush

WINEGLASS, SWIZZLE STICK

Crushed ice
1 oz Kiwi Lime (page 75)
1 oz Elderflower Blush (page 164)
4 oz fresh grapefruit juice
Slice of kiwi

Fill the glass with ice. Add the Kiwi Lime, Elderflower Blush, and grapefruit juice; stir. Garnish with kiwi slice.

Ancho Sunset

Liquid Sunshine

OLD-FASHIONED GLASS, SWIZZLE STICK

2   ice cubes
2   oz Sunny Splash (page 102)
3   oz fresh orange juice
    Splash of ginger ale
    Twist of orange peel

Put the ice cubes in the glass. Add the
Sunny Splash, orange juice, and ginger
ale; stir. Garnish with orange twist.

Pumpkin Spice

MUG, SWIZZLE STICK

1   tsp cinnamon sugar
    Pinch of coarse sea salt
2   oz Pumpkin Pie (page 100)
4   oz warm apple cider
    Cinnamon stick

Mix the cinnamon sugar and sea salt.
Wet the rim of the mug and coat with
mixture. Add the Pumpkin Pie and cider;
stir. Garnish with cinnamon stick.

SIDECAR/SOUR

LIQUEUR SPIRIT + SOUR

Whiskey Sours, a mixture of whiskey, sugar, and lemon juice, have been around
nearly as long as Old-Fashioneds. Some say they hit their pinnacle of sophistication with the development of the Sidecar at the Ritz Hotel in Paris, with brandy
replacing the whiskey and sweet orange liqueur stepping in for sugar.

Capsaicin Cocktail

CHILLED COCKTAIL GLASS, COCKTAIL SHAKER

    Ice cubes
2   oz Ancho Mescal (page 220)
1   oz Sweet-Pepper Surprise (page 80)
½   oz fresh lime juice
    Wedge of lime

Fill the shaker with ice. Add the Ancho Mescal, Sweet-
Pepper Surprise, and lime juice; shake. Wait for 1 minute;
shake again; strain into the glass. Garnish with lime wedge.

Cardamom Sidecar

CHILLED COCKTAIL GLASS, COCKTAIL SHAKER

    Ice cubes
2   oz bourbon
1   oz Ginger-Cardamom Mead (page 115)
1   oz fresh lemon juice
    Slice of fresh or pickled ginger

Fill the shaker with ice. Add the bourbon, Ginger
Cardamom Mead, and lemon juice; shake. Wait for 1 minute;
shake again; strain into the glass. Garnish with ginger slice.

Orange-Almond Sour, 252

Italian Kamikaze

CHILLED SHOT GLASS, COCKTAIL SHAKER

	Ice cubes
1½	oz Finocchio (page 96)
¼	oz Anisette (page 107)
¼	oz fresh orange juice
	Twist of orange peel

Fill the shaker with ice. Add the Finocchio, Anisette, and orange juice; shake; strain into the glass. Garnish with orange twist.

L'Orange

CHILLED COCKTAIL GLASS, COCKTAIL SHAKER

	Ice cubes
2	oz Clear Orange (page 58)
1	oz fresh orange juice
	Dash of orange bitters
	Twist of orange peel

Fill the shaker with ice. Add the Clear Orange, orange juice, and bitters, and shake. Wait for 1 minute; shake again; strain into the glass. Garnish with orange twist.

Mango Colada

GOBLET, BLENDER

2	cups crushed ice
3	oz Tropical Orchid (page 124)
2	oz canned coconut milk
¼	oz fresh lime juice
	Sliver of vanilla bean or twist of lime

Put the ice in the blender and add the Tropical Orchid, coconut milk, and lime juice; process until blended and thick. Garnish with a sliver of vanilla bean or lime twist.

Niçoise

HIGHBALL GLASS, COCKTAIL SHAKER

	Ice cubes
2	oz Tomato Essence (page 94)
1	oz Provençal (page 110)
3	oz fresh orange juice
	Fresh basil sprig

Fill the shaker with ice. Add the Tomato Essence and Provençal and shake; strain into the glass. Put 2 ice cubes in the glass and add the orange juice. Garnish with basil.

Orange-Almond Sour

OLD-FASHIONED GLASS, COCKTAIL SHAKER

	Ice cubes
2	oz Sweet Almond (page 134)
2	oz orange juice
1	oz fresh lemon juice
½	orange slice
	Maraschino cherry

Fill the shaker with ice. Add the Sweet Almond, orange juice, and lemon juice, and shake; strain into the glass. Garnish with orange slice and cherry.

Streamlined Margarita

OLD-FASHIONED GLASS, COCKTAIL SHAKER

1	tsp fleur de sel
	Ice cubes
4	oz Lime Agave (page 63)
½	oz Clear Orange (page 58)
	Wedge of lime

Wet the rim of the glass and coat with fleur de sel. Fill the shaker with ice. Add the Lime Agave and Clear Orange and shake. Wait 1 minute; shake again; strain into the glass. Garnish with lime wedge.

STINGER

LIQUEUR SPIRIT, AROMATICS

These compact but potent cocktails are little more than brandy or whiskey spiked with a shot of liqueur. They are strong and short; perfectly suited to warm the body on a chilly evening.

Harvest Stinger

CHILLED COCKTAIL GLASS, COCKTAIL SHAKER

Ice cubes
2 oz Apple Brandy (page 32)
1 oz Fragrant Fig Mead (page 72)
2 paper-thin apple slices

Fill shaker with ice. Add the Apple Brandy and Fragrant Fig Mead and shake. Wait 1 minute; shake again; strain into the glass. Garnish with apple slices.

Mother Superior

BRANDY SNIFTER, SWIZZLE STICK

1½ oz Toasted Hazelnut (page 138)
1 tsp honey
2 whole cloves
1 twist of lemon peel
Hot water

Combine the Toasted Hazelnut, honey, cloves, and lemon peel in the snifter; stir to dissolve the honey. Add hot water to taste.

Spiced Red Wine

WINEGLASS, SWIZZLE STICK

1½ oz Chai-namon (page 176)
4 oz fruity red wine, like Merlot or Shiraz
Cinnamon stick

Mix the Chai-namon and wine in the glass. Garnish with cinnamon stick.

Harvest Stinger

TONIC

LIQUEUR SPIRIT, SODA, BITTERS (OPTIONAL)

Gin and tonic, the prototypical tonic cocktail, was introduced by the army of the East India Company in India as a way of making quinine (the ultra-bitter treatment for malaria) more palatable. Tonics are similar in structure to coolers, except that they usually contain a bittering agent and/or a slice of lime for garnish. Like coolers, they are associated with warm-weather refreshment.

Black Velvet Redux

CHILLED FLUTE GLASS

- 2 oz Tippling Brown Sugar (page 211)
- ½ oz Hop Blossom (page 163)
- 4 oz chilled Champagne

Combine the Tippling Brown Sugar and Hop Blossom in the glass. Slowly add the Champagne.

Blue Lavender

HIGHBALL GLASS, SWIZZLE STICK

- 12 frozen blueberries
- 2 ice cubes
- 2 oz Lavender Harmony (page 152)
- 4 oz seltzer
  Slice of lime

Put the blueberries and ice cubes in the glass. Add the Lavender Harmony and seltzer; stir. Garnish with lime slice.

Pomegranate Negroni, 255

Caramel Mule

HIGHBALL GLASS, SWIZZLE STICK

> Ice cubes
> 2 oz Caramel Cordial (page 204)
> 4 oz ginger ale
> 3 dashes of bitters, such as Angostura
> 1 caramel candy
> Wedge of lime

Fill glass with ice. Add Caramel Cordial, ginger ale, and bitters; stir. Garnish with candy and lime wedge.

CelRay Tonic

HIGHBALL GLASS, SWIZZLE STICK

> Ice cubes
> 3 oz CelRay Surprise (page 99)
> 4 oz seltzer
> ¼ oz fresh lime juice
> Small celery stalk with leaves

Fill glass with ice. Add CelRay Surprise, seltzer, and lime juice; stir. Garnish with celery.

La Varenne

HIGHBALL GLASS, SWIZZLE STICK

> Ice cubes
> 3 oz Herb-Santé (page 108)
> 4 oz tonic
> Dash of citrus bitters
> Star anise

Fill glass with ice. Add Herb-Santé, tonic, and bitters; stir. Garnish with star anise.

Mint and Soda

HIGHBALL GLASS, SWIZZLE STICK

> Ice cubes
> 2 oz Garden Mint (page 86)
> 4 oz seltzer
> Slice of cucumber
> Fresh mint sprig

Fill glass with ice. Add Garden Mint and seltzer; stir. Garnish with cucumber and mint.

Pomegranate Negroni

HIGHBALL GLASS, SWIZZLE STICK

> Ice cubes
> 4 oz Pom-Pom (page 67)
> 4 oz seltzer
> Slice of lime

Fill glass with ice. Add Pom-Pom and seltzer; stir. Garnish with lime slice.

Rose Spritzer

WINEGLASS, SWIZZLE STICK

> 1 ice cube
> 3 oz Rose-Sauternes Cordial (page 155)
> 4 oz seltzer
> Twist of lemon peel

Put the ice cube in the glass. Add the Rose Sauternes Cordial and seltzer; stir. Garnish with lemon twist.

Rüt Beer Float

HIGHBALL GLASS, COCKTAIL SHAKER, STRAW

> Ice cubes
> 2 oz Rüt (page 83)
> 4 oz seltzer
> 1 scoop vanilla ice cream

Fill shaker with ice. Add the Rüt and seltzer and shake; strain into the glass, filling it two-thirds full. Top with ice cream and stir briefly; serve with a straw.

Sloe Gin Fizz

HIGHBALL GLASS, SWIZZLE STICK

> Ice cubes
> 1 oz Prunelle (page 73)
> 1 oz dry gin
> 4 oz seltzer
> Slice of orange

Fill glass with ice. Add Prunelle, gin, and seltzer; stir. Garnish with orange slice.

Tequila and Tonic
HIGHBALL GLASS, SWIZZLE STICK

    Ice cubes
2 oz Grapefruit Tonic (page 65)
1 oz Lime Agave (page 63)
4 oz tonic
    Twist of grapefruit peel

Fill glass with ice. Add Grapefruit Tonic, Lime Agave, and tonic; stir. Garnish with grapefruit twist.

Tummy Tamer
HIGHBALL GLASS, SWIZZLE STICK

    Ice cubes
2 oz Chamomile Angel (page 158)
4 oz tonic
    Twist of lemon peel

Fill glass with ice. Add Chamomile Angel and tonic; stir. Garnish with lemon twist.

Twisted Horse's Neck
HIGHBALL GLASS, SWIZZLE STICK

    Ice cubes
1 oz Ginger-Cardamom Mead (page 115)
1 oz brandy
4 oz ginger ale
    Twist of lemon peel

Fill glass with ice. Add Ginger-Cardamom Mead and brandy; stir. Pour in ginger ale. Garnish with lemon twist.

RESOURCES

Almost all of the ingredients in these recipes are commonly available in well-stocked liquor and grocery stores. A few things might be harder to find. Mail-order sources are listed below for these.

CINCHONA BARK
(1-ounce to 1-pound bags)

> *www.store.healingifts.com*

CINCHONA BARK POWDER
(1-pound bags)

> **HealthyVillage.com**
> Herbal Advantage, Inc.
> 800-753-9199
> *www.healthyvillage.com*

DRIED FLOWERS
(1-ounce to 4-ounce packages)

> **Herbiary**
> 215-238-9938
> *http://herbiary.com*

INDEX

Also by Andrew Schloss

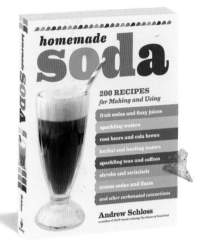

Homemade Soda

Make a wide assortment of delicious carbonated beverages using simple techniques and inexpensive ingredients.

336 PAGES. PAPER. ISBN 978-1-60342-796-8.

OTHER STOREY TITLES YOU WILL ENJOY

Brewing Made Easy by Joe Fisher and Dennis Fisher

A foolproof starters' guide to brewing great beer at home — includes step-by-step instructions and 25 recipes.

104 PAGES. PAPER. ISBN 978-1-61212-138-3.

Homemade Root Beer, Soda & Pop by Stephen Cresswell

More than 60 traditional and modern recipes for fabulous, fizzy creations.

128 PAGES. PAPER. ISBN 978-1-58017-052-9.

Hot Sauce! by Jennifer Trainer Thompson

More than 30 recipes to make your own, plus 60 more recipes for cooking with homemade or commercial sauces.

192 PAGES. PAPER. ISBN 978-1-60342-816-3.

Tasting Beer by Randy Mosher

The first comprehensive guide to tasting, appreciating, and understanding the world's best drink — craft beers.

256 PAGES. PAPER. ISBN 978-1-60342-089-1.

These and other books from Storey Publishing are available wherever quality books are sold or by calling 1-800-441-5700. Visit us at *www.storey.com* or sign up for our newsletter at *www.storey.com/signup*.